A Single Guy's Guide to Predatory Women

Navigating Survival, Heartbreak,
and the media matrix

Vol 1. of the Lipstick and War Crimes Series

by Ray Songtree

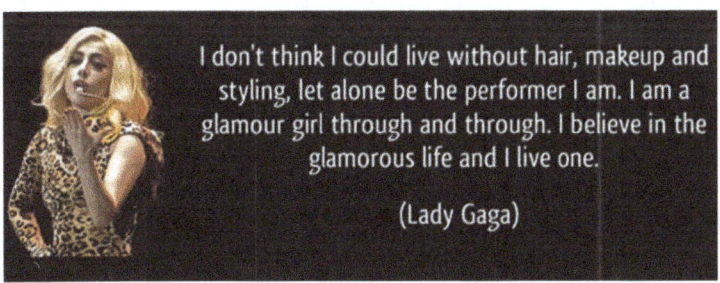

I don't think I could live without hair, makeup and styling, let alone be the performer I am. I am a glamour girl through and through. I believe in the glamorous life and I live one.

(Lady Gaga)

She believes in over consumption. She believes in vanity.
She spreads it to the populace and is supported in doing so.
Over consumption is based on taking
from others, who are left without enough.
This is enforced by the military. Vanity leads to violence.
Lipstick and War Crimes

Kauai Transparency Initiative International

Since we are all psychic, there is no such thing as intellectual property. Intellectual property is an oxymoron. The two words do not combine to make a rational statement because the intellect has no form, and property allegedly does. What intellectual property could mean is we don't want others to take advantage of our work. It can also mean that a for-profit corporation registers whatever it wants and claims it has the legal right to restrict access. In this way nature and even creativity is being commodified. The law is based on an oxymoron.

The author makes no claim to own any concepts in this writing, nor any of the images. The intent of this writing is educational and all revenues will go back into the promotion of education through non-profit Kauai Transparency Initiative International. The use of possibly copyrighted material for critique or eduction comes under "Fair Use" in accordance with, Title 17 U.S.C. Section 107 of the US Copyright Law. For more information go to: http://www.law.cornell.edu/uscode/17/107.shtml. If you wish to use copyrighted material from this book for purposes of your own, that go beyond 'fair use,' you must obtain permission from the copyright owner. Otherwise, portions of this book may be used for non-profit distribution as per Creative Commons License.

I urge the reader to purchase books from which excerpts were taken. See endnotes.

Although the author and publisher have made every effort to ensure that the information in this writing was correct at press time, the author and publisher do not assume and hereby disclaim any liability to any party for any loss, damage, or disruption caused by errors or omissions, whether such errors or omissions result from negligence, accident, or any other cause.

Mission Statement: Kauai Transparency Initiative International believes that human nature is loving. "Right to know" leads to informed choice which leads to local stewardship. When government and industry are honest and open with citizens and consumers, people will naturally choose health for themselves and future generations. A mother protects her child. KTII exists to help causes that work for transparency and disclosure. The goal is an informed loving society on Kauai and afar, brought about by tipping society toward responsible awareness through honest education.
KTII was founded by Ray Songtree in 2011.

To make tax-deductible donations, to inquire about affiliate programs
or for speaking/workshop/concert inquiries, see KTII.org

Lipstick and War Crimes by Ray Songtree is licensed
under a Creative Commons Attribution-NonCommercial
4.0 International License.

A Single Guy's Guide to Predatory Women, Vol. 1 ISBN 978-1-941293-29-4 Paperback
A Single Guy's Guide to Predatory Women, Vol. 1, Epub ISBN 978-1-941293-30-0 Electronic book

Beneath this flame

    the melting candle inside me

Before me,

    your pearl eyes

Your elegant skin

    caressing

    the light of my mind

– Ray Songtree 1976

Thank you Mom, Ontshauwan, Penny, Diana, and Riza

Volume 1 of the *Lipstick and War Crimes Series* by Ray Songtree has been published with different covers and different introductions for different demographic groups. This is not about money, it is about tipping diverse groups towards balance with their ecologies, by abandoning an artificial heartless globalist technocracy. *Zen and the Art of De-programming* has Buddhist, Christian, and Indigenous introductions included. *Begging Faith* has Christian introduction. *Indigenous Re-call* has indigenous intro. *A Thinking Girl's Guide to Sexual Identity* (students), *Feminism Revisited*, *She Promised Me Paradise* (Hawaiian souvenir edition) and *Lipstick and War Crimes* editions are available also as Vol. 1 (they have no introduction.) The Zen edition is the most comprehensive. Bulk or wholesale rates are available on bookstore page at Lipstick-and-War-Crimes.org. Translation or affiliate ideas welcomed. Contact www.KTII.org

Caste of Characters in Vol. 1: "Mother of Feminism" CIA agent Gloria Steinem, Miley Cyrus, Jane Fonda, Albert Einstein, Madonna, Obama and his true father, Shirley McClain, lesbian Katherine Hepburn, Henry Kissinger, secret elitist Oprah Winfrey, Alice Walker, CIA Hugh Hefner, Kate Upton, Warren Beatty, Katy Perry, Soviet defector Yuri Bezmenov, Hillary Clinton, Beyoncé Knowles, Papua New Guinea, Jay-Z, Marilyn Monroe, Gaga, Warren Buffet, Shakira, Kristina Aguilera, Hero Cathy O'Brien, Fukashima, Pharrell Williams, Angelina Jolie, Bill Gates, Elizabeth Taylor, Nelson Mandela, and your mind...

Vol. 2 Editions. Student, Christian, Zen, Jewish, India, and Jennifer Lopez editions. All volumes in series are stand alone, however, Vol 2 is the most historical and encompassing. Find E-books online. Search "Ray Songtree." All these editions are the same book with different introductions.
The Spanish edition is called *Lápiz Labial & Crímenes de Guerra*.

Christian, Zen and Indigenous Introductions

Christian Introduction

Christian, Zen and Indigenous Introductions

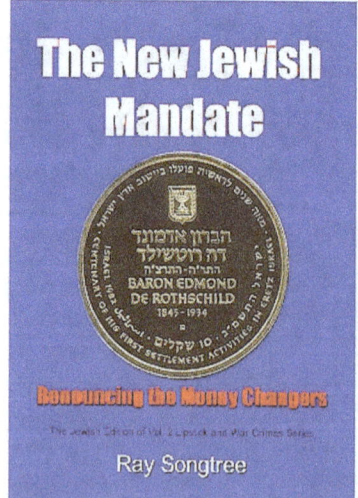
Jewish Introduction for friends and critics of Israel

Introduction for India Black and White interior

Christian and Indigenous Introductions

Volume 1, Ignoring The Future and Looking Fabulous

Vol. 3 is called *Henry and Beyoncé* He an exalted mk-ultra handler and she an exalted victim. (Vol. 1) Both are cogs of same machine to entrance and trick us. Vol. 3 deprograms the origins of followship. "Progress" has no realistic goal. Beyoncé's "Billionaire Girl's Club" dumbs us down.

Superbowl Halftime Show - Beyonce,

"Ignoring the future and looking fabulous"

Above foreground, severely wounded Richard Larry Weaver. Below, author Ray Songtree and *USS Liberty* survivor, Richard Larry Weaver, who discovered that the submarine *USS Amberjack* fired a torpedo and hit his ship in the infamous false flag attack of June 8, 1967 off the Gaza coast that was blamed solely on Israel. (Israel and U.S. receive orders from the exact same globalists.) Larry has had 36 surgeries. The Great Mystery arranged our meeting. Larry's Mother-in-Law and my Mom were friends at an elderly accommodations on Maui.

I include these photos of Richard Larry Weaver to honor and thank him for his investigation and to acknowledge the mysterious spirit that brought us together for our common work of seeking truth and justice. Larry does not endorse all views in the series. The reader can hear his radio interview at link below.

https://lipstick-and-war-crimes.org/1967-uss-liberty-attacked-by-submarine-uss-amberjack-crew-member-blows-whistle/

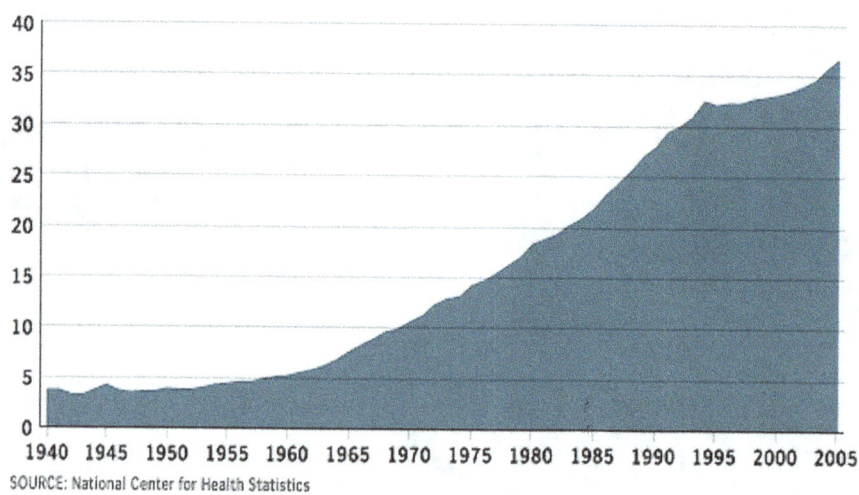

Percent of Total Births in the United States to Unmarried Women, 1940-2005
SOURCE: National Center for Health Statistics

> *Strangers in the night exchanging glances*
> *Wondering in the night*
> *What were the chances*
> *we'd be sharing love*
> *Before the night was through ...*

Frank Sinatra 1966. Scripted Hollywood social engineering; sports sex without commitment as the new normal.

Please check out my first Youtube, "The Illuminati Beast Turns a New Leaf."
Ray Songtree, Kauai Transparency Initiative

Introduction to

A Single Guy's Guide to Predatory Women

This is the male student's mirror edition of *Thinking Girls Guide to Sexual Identity*. In fact, it is the same book.

There is little difference in how a man finds a good woman or a woman finds a good man. First of all you have to be one or the other and not some mix. You have to know what you are. You need to be clear because a good woman is not going to go for someone who is not quality. You have to be a good to find goodness. You have to know what purity is and practice it. Drinking beer and farting is not going to impress a good woman, just as dressing like a slut is not going to impress you. You have to see beyond the cute raw energy or the voluptuous magnetism, which is difficult, but if you don't see beyond and soul search the tone and voice of a perspective mate, you will get burnt and the burn doesn't go away. A scar is a scar. There is a saying in India, "It is better to walk alone than to walk with fools."

When we spend any time with someone, we are investing our energy. Be careful. Believe me, there are heaps of young women who know this instinctively and who feel the same as you or I. In the slowness of courtship, you should get to know several women, just because you like them, without getting addicted to something physical with any of them. Your dates should not be solo, they should be with her friends. Then you will get to know who she is when she isn't on her best behavior. Natural, not artificial. If you can meet her parents and just be friends, you will be years ahead and the long road may open for you. And that long road may be a long friendship, which is plenty. Before you kiss her, find out what ALL her behaviors are. This takes time, but you are walking on ice. If you don't walk softly, you will fall through and the river will drown you in sorrow or make you tough and hard and fxxked up.

If you meet someone who is proud of her bisexual play, she will be damaged for life. The pride means she actually subverted her own natural femininity, the divine feminine, the natural feminine which I discuss more in Vol. 2. Since bisexual experimentation is on the rise, and obviously being promoted by the same media that controls our news, any thoughtful man would ask what the hell is going on? Why is this being promoted? That is why I wrote this non-profit book series, to unravel the conundrum. (Non-profit means I will not make a dime. This is my service to spirit and Earth and it is free, but of course, there are many expenses to producing anything.) I suggest that you stay away from mixed up people and find someone clear and whole. Perhaps in this country there are still virgins in the religious communities. There you might find a good wife who can give you her whole heart, not a left over damaged shard of broken glass.

If you feel broken yourself, don't go on the rebound with another relationship. Vision quest is taking the time to come to quietude and inner vision, alone. If you are not clear, you won't find someone clear.

Another huge uphill battle young men face is that half the women you meet did not experience a committed full time father. They really don't know how to be a wife. And half of male readers here don't have a husband or father role model either.

As humans we have a pure nature. Original sin is a lie coming out of fourth century Rome. You are a being of clear light with karmic habits. That is what you are. You will never be free of karmic habits but they can be closer to light than to habit. Responsibility in serving others will teach you what it means to be a man, and your children will teach you how to be a dad, but let them be your teachers. Since you may have no father role model, you will need to dig deep into your essence to be a really good dad. As heart breaking as it is to see your kids grow up and no longer need you, the best thing you will ever do is to try to be a good parent. Look forward to it! And being an uncle or an adopted Big Brother is huge.

This first Volume of the Lipstick and War Crimes series will clue you into who is engineering our values and why. It is orchestrated, it is organized, it has a source, and it has a goal. It will require several volumes to wrap your head around. It took me years, but it could take you just weeks. That is why I wrote this. I want you to analyze it yourself, but I will give young men here in Volume 1, a glimpse into what has shaped the women that make up your peers.

Young women who happen to read this, remember, most people worldwide, only two generations ago, lived in rural indigenous cultures where women never tried to look sexy. Looking sexy is a vanity, a whoredom, foisted on urban women, and now all women. You don't need it at all. No matter what, if you are clean and tidy, you are attractive. This is a world wide truth, and through the ages. Fresh flowers always look great :) Beauty wilts and rust rusts, but beauty is beauty and fresh flowers don't need makeup.

When I was in high school in 60's, a bit young to understand Woodstock Festival, devastated by the murder of Robert F. Kennedy, sports sex was already in vogue. However, then, it was discreet. Now it is on the street, and inhibition is called "shy shit" by the band Maroon 5.

We are conditioned now NOT to save something special for someone special. We are expected by everyone around us to give away our tenderness, our sweetness, our hearts, our hopes, our strength to anyone with something wet for our need. The heart doesn't even matter for the icons profiled in the pages you are about to read.

You will also find out why there are at least 22 American men, who were in the military, who take their own lives every single day. The military did not make them real men, it made them broken men. Again, we have to ask what the hell is going on? These brothers were lied to and no one supported them in recovering from the lie. Instead, the lie surrounded them. False pride, my country right or wrong, keeps them in a cold lonely corner. Their suffering is denied and ignored, exactly like the radiation coming to West Coast from Fukashima is ignored. Non sequitur? Keep reading. Our entire civilization is based on "take the money and run and don't look back." You, the reader, are going to change that by becoming a good man. The lie in our imperialistic nation is that being involved with war crimes is heroic. Will you support the lie?

If you know a veteran who is proud of his service, buy him the book, *War is a Racket* by General Smedley Butler. It is plain foolery to be proud of being used and screwed. Ripping off the world is not going to continue as the future for the United States. We will bring the jobs home and we will bring the troops home. The enemy are the war profiteers who create war and fund both sides. They also produced the slut role models with their money. This money trail is clear in Vol. 2.

The same grief, that veterans experience and hide, is what women experience who have given away their bodies. They committed love crimes. Lipstick and war crimes. One reason the singer Adele is popular with women is she sings about grief. We have a heart broken society and this is not "progress," it is not good, it is not happy. And this was engineered.

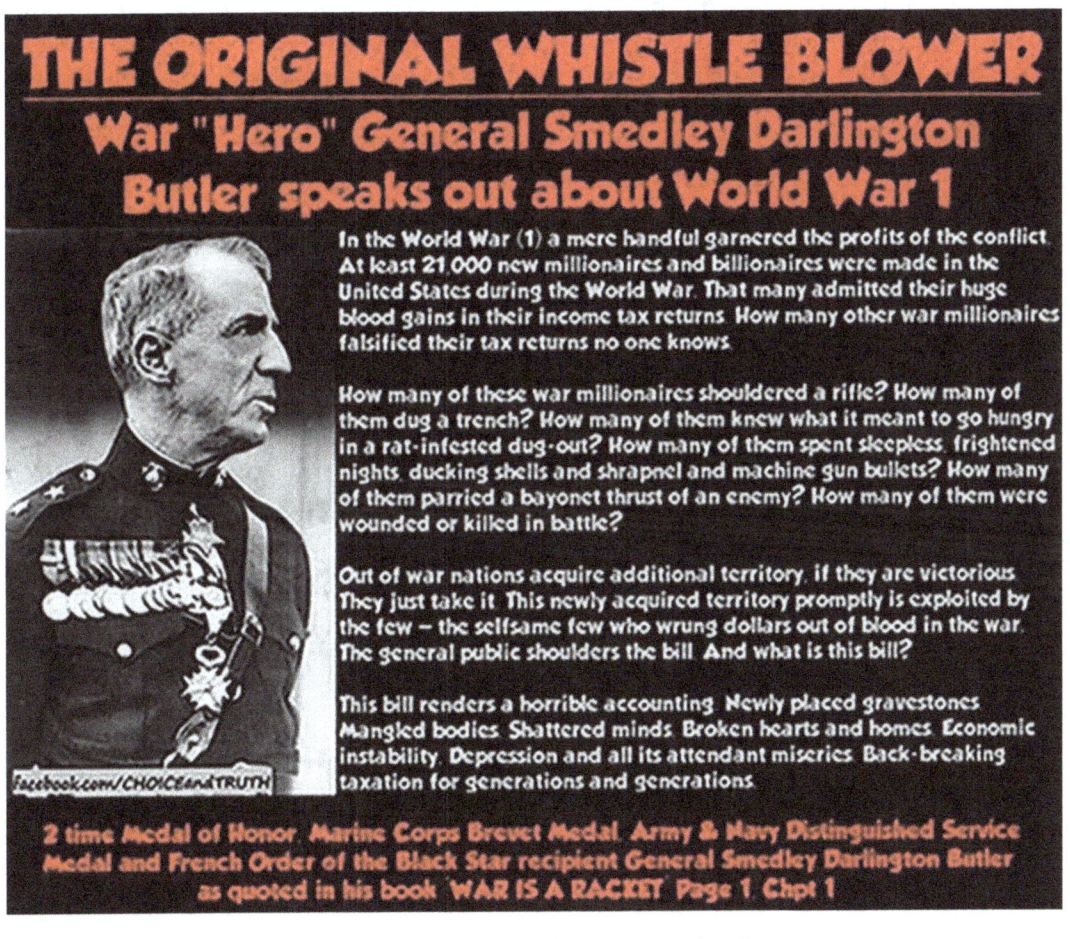

My mom is 95. One hundred years is not that long ago.

On the front cover of this book we see the risque new normal of slutism, with a background of girls at a concert screaming to see their role models, who influence them to become trash. In my opinion, all these diva women are trashy human beings who have sold their soft, tender, sweet souls to the music industry. They can laugh on their way to the bank, and sob in secret the rest of their lives.

To right: anti-nature. What a joke that a man would surrender like this. Look, his arms are paralyzed:) But foolish young women take it seriously, and have become disconnected and predatory.

We do not regain innocence. I am a good person, but my innocence has been broken. I have a big heart. A big broken heart. I know young men who hardly have a heart anymore. I have been with prostitutes. I needed the connection and masturbating wasn't the connection. But I found out how dysfunctional and crazy these people were. Most were single mom's by the way. They became single moms by not following their tradition, but followed the slut role models on front cover. Illegitimate children was one of the goals of the "sexual revolution," though at this point in your study, this seems unbelievable. To find out *Playboy* and *Ms.* magazines were run by CIA is rather shocking. I found young women who were for hire, lying to themselves, exactly like the women you will read about here in Volume 1, who are now the most famous women in the world. They are rich liars. They are rich prostitutes. Like Beyoncé in photo above, they live in a lie of vanity and are surrounded by such people. They are exactly like most politicians. They are vetted and groomed the same way. I don't mean this figuratively. I mean that most politicians have sold their soul just like the entertainment puppets, and jumped through criminal hoops to become well known. As we will learn, the same puppet masters intertwine pop puppet celebrities with political puppet celebrities. They promote each other and hide the stink of each other. One becomes respectable, and the other cool. Some sing and some read teleprompters.

The goal for most people is to become a rich liar and to close one eye to the truth so they can live with half truths and double standards. Consumerism ignores collateral damage.

These words to song written by Glen Ballard and Siedah Garrett nail it. The "Man in the Mirror" version by Noah on Youtube is excellent. Michael Jackson was many things. Please see his Youtube, "They Don't Care About Us"—prison version.

> *I'm gonna make a change*
> *For once in my life*
> *It's gonna feel real good*
> *Gonna make a difference*
> *Gonna make it right*
>
> *As I, turn up the collar on my favorite winter coat*
> *This wind is blowing my mind*
> *I see the kids in the streets with not enough to eat*
> *Who am I to be blind, pretending not to see their needs?*

A summer disregard, a broken bottle top
And a one man soul
They follow each other on the wind ya' know
'Cause they got nowhere to go
That's why I want you to know ...

I've been a victim of a selfish kind of love
It's time that I realize
That there are some with no home, not a nickel to loan
Could it be really me, pretending that they're not alone?

A willow deeply scarred, somebody's broken heart
And a washed-out dream
They follow the pattern of the wind ya' see
'Cause they got no place to be
That's why I'm starting with me

I'm starting with the man in the mirror
I'm asking him to change his ways
And no message could have been any clearer
If you want to make the world a better place
Take a look at yourself, and then make a change

I am asking all readers to take this song personally. We are going to see the sh*t hit the fan.

I have had two broken marriages and a child from each. If you are a young man, I would like you to learn from my mistakes. Wisdom is remembered mistakes, and I offer that.

In the future I may do workshops with young men. We can talk about the male principal and the duty of being a male of the species *Homo sapiens*. It would probably be better if we do this on a group camping trip together. We can talk about Vision Quest. We can talk about the oversoul and grace. We can talk about right livelihood, because, guys, there will be less and less jobs out there as machines take over or supply lines go bankrupt. Most of you with any brains will leave the city, learn to grow things, and become Earthy soulful humans again or you won't survive. The women who are ready to live simply again, are few and far between, but the smart ones, the grounded ones, the soulful ones with connection, will drop the vanity and seek life. The people who want death can stay in the cities. None of us will have a choice when it comes to poverty. Resource depletion is here, and learning to live with less will be liberating for all the addicts of consumerism.

Here is a clue that I would like you to consider ...

There is actually nothing equal about men and women except our loneliness.

> **About the Front Cover**
>
> Shakira – Covered extensively in Vol. 3
>
> Beyoncé – Vol. 1, 2, 3
>
> Miley Cyrus – Vol. 1, 2
>
> Katy Perry – Vol. 1, 2
>
> Nicki Minaj – Vol. 2
>
> Jennifer Lopez – Vol. 2
>
> Christina Aguilera – Vol. 2
>
> Madonna – Vol. 1, 2
>
> Gaga – Vol. 2
>
> Rihanna – Vol. 2
>
> plus many others like Hillary Clinton.

March 26, 2016: Alicia Keyes and Miley Cyrus will enable more Illuminati social engineering by being judges on *The Voice*. Cyrus will present one of her appealing, intelligent, mind controlled split personality alters. This respectability will make her lack of modesty or discretion more acceptable to millions of teens, thereby splitting them and opening them to glory of predatory sports sex. Illuminati NBC wants more fatherless kids and broken hearts. Resist!

A Single Guy's Guide to Predatory Women

Navigating Heartbreak, Survival, and the Media Matrix

On "Yahoo Questions" the following question was asked:
"Why are most women such whores these days?"

"When I go out I see women dressed in short little skirts, tattoos all over their body. They go out and go home with guys they do not even know. Now I noticed heaps of guys these days, just think most women are sluts who will just go to bed with them. Why would a women want to let a guy just use her like that? Why would they enjoy going to bed with some one they do not even know? I think it is just wrong."

"Some people might see me as a slut because I go out and talk to heaps of guys, even let them buy me drinks. My dancing is even a little slutty but when I go out I never let people touch me, or I never go home with any guys"

"It is like people think it is cool to be this way. Its like the new in thing. What happened to people wanting to have a relationship, or at least getting to know some one first?"

Patriotism below the waist. Irrational. Addicted.

The image to left demonstrates the constant bombardment of indulgent, no commitment, sports sex. The byline "Kate Upton—The Newest Reason to Love Your Country" with Upton doing oral on red, white, and blue shows us lipstick and war crimes. If Kate Upton loved life itself, she might not love that her country, the U.S., is dominating and murdering others with 55,000 special ops over seas. (See Glossary *military*) If she loved modesty and purity she wouldn't be on a magazine cover like this. One supports the other. Feminine corruption and masculine corruption. Lipstick and War Crimes.

What do sexual morays have to do with rising incidence of autism, environmental problems, 47 million Americans on food stamps, obesity, the drought in California, foreign policy, 12 year old occupation of Iraq (now by "contractors"), 22 military veterans a day committing suicide, party politics, GMO labeling or the lack of jobs for college graduates? It seems to be a completely isolated worry, but it is not.

The crisis here is not disconnected from the crisis there, as the same culture is manifesting both. Not only are all these problems related but the seriousness of these problems are hidden by an organized Media that entrances and pollutes us at the same time. Who or what is this organization?

Interestingly, the solution to all these problems, including the Media, is the same solution, and the reader will be instrumental in manifesting this solution. The top is corrupt and the bottom is within us.

Mark my words, each of us are going to insist on virtue.

* * *

Hi Ray,

I had to turn off the Katy Perry show; even though it was proving everything you had written, the acts got increasingly worse and I couldn't stomach it anymore. In front of all the kids in the audience, she "gave a shout out" to all the parents who were drinking and feeling tipsy. Then she sang a song about "That's how we do it." That was after singing one called "By the grace of god." When she came out dressed as a toddler asking "Can I be your teenage dream?" and writhing on the stage with her cleavage everywhere, I got that pedophilia is being sold faster than cell phones, and turned it off. Ugh.

– Kathy

Katy Perry is exposed in a later image in Vol. 1 as an actual slave. I would ask the reader to ponder how you might guide a teenager who came to you with the question as to why women are now acting like whores. Please take a little time to write out your answer. I'm curious if your answer will be different when you finish the book. The reason is the same reason that the U.S. is the biggest war criminal in history, according to Nelson Mandela, just to give you a clue.

* * *

Not only is our nightly news skewed as propaganda, but so is our school curriculums and advertisements. This was organized in a very careful manner for about a century now (Vol. 2). None of the manipulation of values by those with the funds to do so, was altruistic. It was all done to create a compliant population that would have no where to find guidance, except from the State and it's laws, or worse, from the hypnotizing circus of controlled entertainment.

> "*In our dreams, people yield themselves with perfect docility* to our molding hands. The present education conventions of intellectual *and character* education fade from their minds, and, *unhampered by tradition*, we work our own good will upon a grateful and responsive folk. … The task is simple. We will organize children and teach them in a perfect way the things their fathers and mothers are doing in an imperfect way."
>
> – John D. Rockefeller Sr. , General Education Board 1906

I hope the reader noticed what he said. He didn't say "my" dreams, he said "our" dreams. Who was organizing what he was discussing? Considering he was very rich and financed by a family known as the Rothschilds who made him rich, and that this family today controls every Central Bank in the world, the reader might now be on guard. Notice also that the training of sound *character* is to be replaced with *docility*. Before the times when the state had so much power, it was human character that upheld society. A docile sheep can't maintain or defend anything.

There is an organization that controls the value of money and can thus control any government, and therefore any culture. This organization wants an "anything goes" non-ethic so they can have free reign. If "anything goes" and there are no taboos, then nothing is "wrong." If people don't have a sense of wrong, they won't fight for what is right or resist tyranny.

Proceed to Account Overview

In the Paypal image to left, a very phony photo shoot, we see the mom with her mouth open, no restraint. That mouth is the most important component of the photo, otherwise the photo would be "boring." What other action is in photo? The mom is wearing gloves so she won't have to touch the Earth. The gloves are made in some factory somewhere in Asia probably, and is polluting the water table. They are made there because of lax environmental laws and because labor prices are kept low by the very banks that establish currency exchange rates. We are looking at the naïve woman, Mary next door, who is destroying the planet. Paypal supports this person, and helps create this person. She is so excited that she doesn't take time to consider the thread of consequences that her lifestyle puts in motion. It is a snap shot of why things are going so badly world wide. We rich are "excited." Mouth open is now seen in most advertisements. If someone is out of control and shouting or laughing loudly, this is supposed to be our goal, our reason to exist. Wow, I want to be excited too! Jaw dropping excited! Wow, let's plant some seeds and open a bank account!

At a recent wedding in Hawaii my elderly mom (94) and I witnessed adults screaming. They were so excited! Grandma has also commented on the way children here scream, including her granddaughter. In no traditional or *indigenous culture* (italics usually means it is glossary term) anywhere, do people behave this way. We have been distracted to seek "excitement" and act unrestrained while not getting our hands dirty with real connection or even paying attention to the sacrifice that comes with real commitment.

"Anything goes" is what "freedom" now means. It means no restraint. When there is no moral order coming from clear restraints that sets up right and wrong within us, what is left is a drunk promiscuous immoral screaming mouth open society. Rather than have inner boundaries that we ourselves maintain as sovereign members of a local community, we are led to accept a police state "for your safety" and have no inner power and no sense of community that we are beholden to. That is, we are "free." Being "free" these days means not being responsible for defining or upholding goodness.

To get to this "anything goes, and nothing is wrong" freedom, that which would make people careful about choices, including a sense of clear inner sexual "orientation," has been systematically dismantled. Any remaining bastion of decency has been attacked. This undermining of identity includes the undermining of expected family roles, and also undermining the idea that service to the community is what normal humans have always done.

The "advanced" "democratic" "free" "developed" nation of UK has become perverted, because "freedom" now means no inner somber commitment to moral guidelines. The outcome or karma is broken homes where children suffer. Nor do children have good role models to re-capture what commitment used to mean. "Adventure" is more important than sacrifice.
Seek "excitement," not commitment! Seek something illicit, not something restrained! Be free!
"Ashley Madison" cheater website Canada—125 million views/month.

In the past, sacrifice for something greater than self was normal. We took care of each other, not me me me. Being selfish and not working for future generations was almost unknown. When I say the past, I am not speaking only about feudal Europe, I am speaking about most of the thousands of cultures before colonization. In the past, only teamwork survived, and anyone who didn't work for the good of the local community was ostracized.

But today, almost no self-regulating communities remain in most places. That is, of course, the goal of globalization, to have global controllers, not local control. The State/Media now defines our responsibilities, and we accept this as sheeple who have little say in the matter. This is very convenient for those who want no responsibility and want to be free, anonymous and illicit. In other words, "freedom" as a sheeple invites temptation without restraint. By feeding the populace wanton desires, the top/down system lowers the chance of resistance to its will.

To dismantle codes of restraint, even religions have been rewritten with CIA operations such as, "A Course In Miracles," (Vol. 2, Chapter 10) that replaces the living spirit behind the New Testament with a programmed head trip that levels all behavior to no sense of responsibility or activism. The teachings of right and wrong have been eliminated and called "traditional." Traditional now means old fashioned, not part of our glorious progress, as in the glorious progress of UK and it's million cheaters above.

How to De-moralize a Society

In the interview [1] paraphrased below, Soviet defector Yuri Bezmenov says 85% of KGB activity was not "007" espionage at all. The larger 85% of activity that the KGB was really involved with is similar to what is occurring in U.S. (1980s). He said it is …

> "a slow process which we call either 'psychological subversion,' or 'active measures,' or 'psychological warfare.' What it basically means is, *to change the perception of reality* of every American to such an extent, that despite the abundance of information, no one is able to come to sensible conclusions in the interests of *defending themselves, their community and their country*. It is a great brainwashing process which goes very slow and is divided into four basic stages."

Stage One – De-moralization: takes 15-20 years to accomplish and is done through "education" via the school system .

In U.S. this is accomplished under the umbrella of pluralism, so that we say "NO!" to nothing, because we are supposed to allow diversity and be tolerant and *not offend anyone by drawing a line*. This is also the reason for irrational immigration. The people who really control government policy, which is absolutely not the elected officials, want a melting pot in which no traditional culture survives. They are very much winning at this point. The "blue" states on on the coasts of the U.S. are populated with very recent immigrants with no loyalty to anything but more entitlements. The "red" states in central U.S. are also recent immigrants, less than 200 years, but more grounded and more conservative because they still have local communities.

Who are "they" that wants a melting pot now in every nation? This series will give you their history and methods. We already got a clue with the insane John D. Rockefeller quote above. What "they" really want is not some noble tolerance of diversity, but rigid homogenization as soon as possible. Diversity will NOT survive under the one umbrella of "equality." In the name of "tolerance" no traditional culture that wants its own unique standards will be tolerated.

In this new non-culture, we politely remain quiet and defend nothing at all. In fact we are trained to say NO to anyone who says NO. "You are being judgmental!" This is our indignant reaction to anyone with a strong opinion. We condemn them as being judgmental. We label them as homophobe or radical or ultra right. We label anyone who has an opinion and smear them with this label or that. How quickly quiet, pseudo-gentle, fair, nice people become sarcastic and vindictive when confronted with new information, as this series tries to offer. In this series, I don't say NO! very often, though I certainly feel it. I point out things the reader might want to examine. Just for presenting this kind of new information, many people try to smear authors and speakers. We have been trained to be sheeple who do not ask questions and resent examination. While professing tolerance, we are taught to hate alternative views and be derisive with anyone who questions the official story.

The idea of "One World" with no unique cultural taboos allowed, is sold under the "lets be fair" lexicon. We are trained in school not to have moral discernment, which requires *the ability to question* in order to make a judgement call. Good judgement is based on conscience, not the "right answer." We are taught to fit in and obey the rules. This kind of morals or ethics is simply taking orders, not *taking responsibility* for what is fair.

We see this occuring whenever a new law is passed and people immediately change their value system to conform. What is legal, this day or that, is what is "right." If the law said people having sex with children is now legal, then many people would simply adapt to the new law and fiercely condemn and smear anyone who disagreed. That's what happened with making discrimination against "sexual orientation" (Vol. 2, Chapter 10) illegal. Suddenly when someone before might have been seen as psychologically unstable, now this same person is supposed to be seen as "equal." This accomplishes the mission that there is no such thing as stable psychology because there is no definition of unstable. If someone dresses like the sex they are not, we are supposed to see them as normal for our children to be around. This is one of the ways a society is dismantled and made docile, a la Rockefeller and friends.

For many people, being "liked" on Facebook is more important than taking a stand that might be considered controversial. In fact, even in their own minds they won't take a stand. This is amazing *social engineering* to create a population like this. We are not taught to discriminate right from wrong, we are taught to no longer use discriminating wisdom. This is the DE-moralization process.

According to Yuri Bezmenov, the government needs to de-moralize an entire generation of kids to be able to accomplish this first stage. This has long been completed in the U.S.

(Yuri didn't mention the depressing government assassinations of JFK, RFK, Malcolm X, and Martin Luther King in just five years, and the un-investigated deaths of world famous Janis Joplin, Jimi Hendrix, and Jim Morrison in one year. Neither Hendrix or Morrison were still doing drugs. Four other people died of something that was given to Joplin. The goal of these synchronized murders of famous stars was to deflate youth and it did.)

Moral scrutiny is personal discriminating wisdom applied to each and every bit of information, in order to weigh if it really is true *in terms of value*. This is the key component to *personal sovereignty* (Glossary, Vol. 2), the weighing of decisions under the scrutiny of conscience. "Does it feel right? Does it feel righteous?"

One cannot even ask these questions, if right and righteousness was never taught as a value, with the contrasting words wrong and sinfulness taught as the taboo.

* * *

Truth is not a fact, truth is a value.

We should be taught that morals are based on value. Morals aren't laws, they are the application of conscience and the personal responsibility to be able to say "NO, this is not okay, this is wrong." For example, if someone feels taking part in war is a moral decision, they might not go to war. If someone thinks that going to war is a legal decision, they might go to war because the law told them to do so.

The mind control of placing "facts" in a child's head, without any moral approval on the part of the child, means the information was never really processed, it was just imprinted into her/his head. If children cannot reject the lesson, the lesson is retarding the child's moral development. People that are educated (all of us) in this unfiltered brainwashing trap will not believe an exposé or even an event when they see it happen with their own eyes, if it runs counter to the "truth" imprinted into them without any moral processing. (We will be introducing traumatic based mind control shortly, where the person or child is so traumatized, a new set of behaviors can be imprinted whole cloth. Boot camp is traumatic mind control. Officers are handlers.)

The reader can show friends and family real evidence, provide documents and pictures, even take them to concentration camps, and they will stick with the imprinted lies from school. This series is not a bunch of beliefs, it is a research guide of evidence. Yet I have had people read this book and ask, "Do you really believe all that?" What they mean is, "I already have the official story belief and this doesn't fit in with that, therefore your evidence can't be real." My re-education was radical and yours will be also. I present a reality we were never told about.

So if we believe that Israel was created by poor refugees from the Nazi gas chambers and then we find out that Israel was created in the 1880s by the Edmond Rothschild, and came into existence because of the Israeli terrorist organizations known as Haganah, the Irgun Zvai Leumi and the

Stern Gang [2], the mind programmed average person's reaction is "I don't believe it." Then, they will smear, as they were taught to do. "You are crazy."

If you show your family and friends that Sir Francis Bacon was the one man who compiled all the disparate 54 translations and wrote the King James version of Bible, and that the English concept of Christianity was thus shaped though the lens of just one man, who just happened to be a 33rd degree Freemason, they won't believe it! [3]

If you show your family and friends that Global Warming was invented by the Rockefeller rich boys' Club of Rome in 1968 [4] and has been debunked by a large group of NASA scientists and even show them the NASA letter [5], they won't believe it!

> "In searching for a new enemy to unite us, *we came up with the idea* that pollution, the threat of global warming, water shortages, famine and the like would fit the bill. In their totality and in their interactions, these phenomena do constitute a common threat which *demands the solidarity of all peoples*. But in designating them as the enemy, we fall into the trap about which we have already warned namely mistaking systems for causes. All these dangers are caused by human intervention and it is only through changed attitudes and behavior that they can be overcome. The real enemy, then, is humanity itself."

As the reader will discover in this series, the real enemy is the Globalists, who want to shape everyone to become docile, who think they have to come up with a top/down idea to trick the masses *into solidarity* under one world government. Yes, human activity has caused massive problems, but who were the captains of industry? And the statement is lying. It is "systems" of hierarchal control that are absolutely the enemy. Human "intervention" is not the cause of environmental destruction. The cause is new industrial impact derived from new materialistic values. The statement never mentions consumption and choice, because the *power to exercise choice* is erased from consideration for the docile sheeple. The Globalists never imagine that informed choice could ignite the genius of the human being.

So the *Roth-efeller* (Glossary) Club of Rome would never empower the masses with the conscience of choice. Rather, they blame "humanity." Which humanity? Should we blame *indigenous people* who are living as they have for thousands of years, or the humanity of over-consumers with no moral restraint as in perverted UK? There is no one humanity! This was another lie in the statement. If The Club of Rome acknowledged there is more than one culture, they again would be empowering choice. They dare not! They are Globalists. All people everywhere on globe need to be in one sheep pen or they won't get their dream. We will meet Cecil Rhodes soon.

If the reader would like to jump ahead, you can go to www.Geoengineeringwatch.org and learn about the many decades long science of weather control to produce the famines and extreme weather to unite us all against "global warming." In a further book in series I will show how the data for global warming models was also invented and that scientific academies and journals are funded or de-funded. [6] Yes, there are too many people, but more important, there are too many unthinking sheeple, and the Globalists created this dumbed down docile population.

If you show your family and friends that the sushi in the store is not safe because of mercury (Vol. 2, Chapter 6) or that fluoride in toothpaste and drinking water has a long history of retarding the brain, or that data shows radiation levels are 60 times higher in San Diego than a year ago [7], they won't believe it!

After the 2010 Gulf of Mexico Oil Spill (Gusher) many people were poisoned and got sick, and their own families refused to believe it was happening. They could not even believe their own eyes. "The nightly news *program* hasn't mentioned this so it cannot be happening."

The ability to examine information with an examining mind was taken out of our education intentionally. To say "I won't go along with this, it feels WRONG" has been taken out of our repertoire of emotions. One has to have a sense that "I decide what is true" to be able to discern truth. That word *true* includes a moral element. "Does this feel right? Or does this feel wrong." If right and wrong are blurred, the sheeple will not know what to think.

So rather than look at new information and see if it might be true/worthwhile, the person planted with ideas that they never scrutinized, just goes into denial when given new information that runs counter to their *programming*. "I don't believe it!" What they really mean is "I already believe something I never questioned, and I have never been trained to question anything and can't." Mission accomplished for Globalists.

What is a Globalist? That is what this series is all about. Though most people refer to the elite 1% of the 1% of the richest most powerful people in world, who are at the very top of the pyramid of abuse, as "Globalists," or the Cabal, or the Illuminati, or the Banksters, we need to consider the bottom of the globalist pyramid that holds them up also. Look in the mirror.

Am I a Globalist?

If you think that there is one answer for "humanity" then you are a globalist. If you even use the word "humanity," then you have been socially engineered with this globalist programming. So when Hero Whistle Blower David Icke says "Humanity get off your knees" he is not getting it yet. Rather, "Local communities, get off your knees!" or "City people get off your knees and return to local communities!" *Indigenous people* don't have to get off their knees. They haven't swallowed the docile sheeple globalist mind control and become utterly dependent yet.

If you are NOT a member of a self-regulating community, then you are a globalist who wants "an answer" for all communities everywhere else, that should be enforced. You think like this because you have no connection with any land, and are landless, and you probably think that all other lands exist so corporations can harvest what they want, so YOU can have variety at the grocery store. Are you a Globalist?

If you believe this, then you might believe in one world government that would crush any people who said no to the corporations such as the Trans-Pacific Partnership (TPP). Are you a Globalist?

If you believe "we are all one" as the New Age Operation has taught you, and that all the world needs One answer, One solution, One plan for "the One future" under "One love," One law, One design, to be administered fairly by a computer, then … Are you a Globalist?

If you think you have the right to travel to any land or any community anywhere, without an invitation, and that no community or nation, has the right to say no to tourism, then what do you respect? Do you disrespect the rights of others to have boundaries because that isn't fair? Do you listen to channeled beings like "the Pleiadians?" Are you a Globalist?

If you believe the 1948 Rothschild Universal Declaration of Human Rights should be applied to thousands of cultures, and that all children should have "free" access to globalist propaganda so we have "fair and equal education," then I must ask, are you a Globalist? Because if you are, you are the bottom of the pyramid that was created to support the top of the pyramid.

By contrast, if you own land and farm or hunt and understand the ecology of your region, you are not a Globalist, you are a Human Being.

If you are a Human Being, you don't think in terms of "the answer for humanity," you think in terms of the sustainability of the land where you live because you love life and want life to continue. You don't know about anyone else's land because that is their business, not yours. You are a steward, not a sheeple. You are a survivor, not someone on rations, at the end of a long supply line, about which you have little control or even comprehension. Rather, as a non-globalist that knows your soil and insects and birds and weather, you also know where your food and water comes from.

As a non-globalist you refuse to work at a factory or mining operation that is polluting the ground water just to make some money. You care about the ground water staying clean forever. So if it was 1977 and foreigners come and build a gold mine on your island called Papua New Guinea (north of Australia, east of Indonesia) and your rivers become poisonous, then you might go with your friends and family and attack and destroy that mine. Of course, you would, because *you know what wrong means*, because this is your land, and the water is the blood of your great grand children's future.

If you want to become a non-globalist, then you put into action that "caring is righteous and not caring is not righteous." Since you are just one person in a big world, your activism starts at home. You start with your own body. You eat pure food. And you educate your friends and family. That is your domain. That is your stewardship. As we say in Hawaii, "That is your kuleana."

> *"The language of my kupuna (ancestor, grandparent, relative or close friend) is a melting pot of meanings. Unlike the English language, the Hawaiian language can say many different things in one word. The word KULEANA, as noted in the Hawaiian dictionary can mean right, privilege, concern, responsibility, etc. But, for me, as a kanaka maoli (native person) KULEANA is not just a word that says responsibility but it is much deeper and richer than what the English language can express.* **It speaks of a value, a way of thinking.**

> *"This is an example of what kuleana means to me ... "It is my kuleana to teach my children and grandchildren their native culture and* **the values and belief** *of our family." If I internalize this statement and agree that as a makua and kupuna (parent and grandparent), my responsibility is to teach my children and grandchildren our culture, values and beliefs of our family, it becomes a goal, a mission, a duty. But, if I add the additional meaning of PRIVILEGE to this statement, the perspective changes to: "how honored am I to be able to have this responsibility of having children and grandchildren to share my knowledge, stories and thoughts" This additional meaning to the word, allows one to truly think about what they are doing, how they are doing it, and to express a gratitude that is sometimes lacking in taking on a responsibility.*

> *"When given a task or responsibility, adjust your perspective to include privilege, the task will take on a new meaning and that is KULEANA."*
>
> – Diane Kamaolipua and Searle Wailana Grace (Gracefulguidance.com)

* * *

What was taken away from us is the idea that some things are wrong, and we better be watching out for it! What was taken out of school was the word "wrong." We wouldn't want to offend anyone!

Without quality control where is the quality? Quality control weeds out the wrong. It means we each have the responsibility to have a sense of what is wrong. If we condemn nothing we aren't peaceful, enlightened, or nice. We are not spiritually balanced or evolved. We are the opposite. We are part of the problem because society and the environment is in deep doo doo. Being nice is not going to cut it, as we face the cliff of our karma as heedless blind consumers.

De-moralization, is not only becoming despondent, but is the intentional *social engineering* by the top of the pyramid Globalists, who control all we sheeple, to try to make us lose faith in morals so that the top of the pyramid gets the future THEY want. We go along because we trust the system because we have to, because we are dependent. The huge realization you may gain from this series is that we trusted our leaders, who were actually tricking us and converting us. It is *through deception* that our futures are being designed by "them". The top of the pyramid doesn't care about the welfare of the bottom of the pyramid, who they use. There is no elite without slaves. Another way to say it is that an empire is never nice.

> *They don't care about us.*
>
> – from the song by Michael Jackson, wrongly framed as a pedophile and murdered for writing songs like this

Now what do "They" think of someone who is strong? For control freaks, they want the masses to be weak, not strong. The top of pyramid hates inner strength. Since strength comes from faith, they hate faith.

De-moralize means to reduce faith in morality. If one believes or has faith in being good, one will be good. If one believes in fidelity, fidelity is possible. If one has no faith in fidelity, infidelity will be easier. To hold to a standard requires faith or morality. Someone with strong faith cannot be de-moralized. They will fight endlessly for good because they have faith.

In order to make us compliant, morals and faith in morals had to be re-molded, so that we wouldn't stand up for goodness against a bad State.

(As you will learn in how I personally feel, I do not believe we need faith in something far away or someone far away. Jesus is not going to erase your karma. You are responsible. Faith is something bigger than someone else. Faith is something we cultivate and is ours. Check out just one example Mathew 9:28. By the way, I am not a Christian in the way most Christians have been taught to be. We can have faith and never have read or heard of any scripture or teaching. When I was in Arnhemland with the Yolgnu people of the north tip of Australia, I met a man who was very obviously a man of faith. I feel that faith is what we naturally can connect with when we are deprogrammed from all the chatter. This is a very Buddhist view, by the way, and also very close to Jesus. Luke 12:27 … "Consider the lilies how they grow: they toil not, nor do they spin, yet I say unto you that Solomon in all his glory was not arrayed like one of these."

Stage Two – Destabilization: Already completed in the U.S. as shown by very little citizen involvement in any issue. The television has helped accomplish this. Spectate, don't do.

Stage Three – Crisis: This period now. As we will learn, the drought in California is a man- made event. I know … you don't believe it! Today, April 29, 2015 Amarillo, Texas experienced the hottest day on record and on the same day, snow falling. This was due to weather warfare under the science of "geo-engineering" using chemtrails and a system called HAARP. [8] I know, you don't believe it! As early as 2001 [9] the U.S. Navy had plans for the ice free waters around arctic circle, that we have had in last few years, because they knew it was scheduled. Geo-engineering is accomplishing the Club of Rome planned crises. I know, you don't believe it!

As of this writing in spring of 2015 a very large military exercise in the southern states is occurring called Jade Helm. This is not a drill. They are mapping out how they will actually take over that part of the country and setting out a map of "human terrain" that could be operational. That is, they are identifying freedom fighters. I know … you don't believe it!

Stage Four – Normalization: after the crisis, the country is officially taken over by a Big Brother Marxist like government, where the leaders 'appear benevolent' and tell us everything has been 'normalized.'

According to Yuri Bezmenov, this process is an ongoing effort and he was surprised when he came to U.S. that the process is further along here than anyone ever imagined could be accomplished in USSR.

We need to find out who organized this. You will understand this by the end of Vol. 2, Chapter 2. If you are balking, and experiencing the programmed reaction "crazy conspiracy," please read the two letters again which we started with and the evidence, not opinion, that UK is now a perverted nation, and start believing it really is happening. It is right in front of your eyes. Start believing what you see and start asking … "Is this righteous?"

THE CRISIS OF THE FEMININE IS EVERYONE'S CRISIS

To understand the crisis of the feminine, which equals the crisis of the environment of the entire Earth, we need to study the power structure that has tried to control the future. If dominance is a male characteristic, the victim has been the feminine itself. And if feminists have been co-opted by this desire to "be on top," then they have only added to the assault.

In my opinion, dominance on the physical plane might have a sexual polarity of men physically stronger than women, but the desire to dominate in the mind is found in all realms and is a problem everywhere. I am speaking of corruption, ego, and lack of compassion found in any realm, in any dimension. I call it vanity, or the *vanity that disconnects* (Glossary). The opposite, by contrast, is quietude, emptiness, humbleness, compassion and empathy, or "connection."

Both genders have an equal chance of falling prey to vanity. In no other way are the two genders equal biologically, emotionally, or energetically. Though the cards we have been given are not the same, we are equal in being imperfect.

The power structure in Western Empire, in our times, has consisted not only of men, but the women who raised these men, from childhood, to be elitist manipulators. These moms were elitist also. They allowed their own children to be mind controlled to become ruthless. And so the series touches psychology also. It has to.

You see, if Karl Marx, a bankster Rothschild employee (I know, you don't believe it! Vol. 2, Chapter 2), had considered that disparity in class structure was rooted, not in greed, but rather initially in the temptation by the mind to feel it is better, more correct, certain and beyond question (which becomes a corrupt authority), then he would have contemplated the role of the Self a bit more. In studying the tendency to feel certain, he would have discovered abuse. "I know The Truth, and you don't, so I am entitled and you aren't!"

Rather than studying capitalist hoarding, with the dream that everyone should be equally materialistic, Marx could have studied purification. But Marx was so deluded by the vanity of being certain, that he could never critique his own thinking. But then, it wasn't his job description to be a visionary. It was his job description to fulfill the script he was paid to recite, which was to create a contrary blame game movement to replace aristocratic slavery with state slavery ... in the name of fairness, of course.

I am saying that primary to class, and primary to patriarchy is self-entitlement, vanity, self importance, and this is the reason there is crime in the world, not a gender conspiracy or any other kind of conspiracy. It is vanity which denies connection. It is certainty that denies spirit. And so Marx was an intellectual idiot who could not see nor understand the purpose of religion.

Sure, the Church warped the message of Jesus and created an opiate of the masses, but why didn't Marx use Jesus's admonition against the rich, "The rich getting to Kingdom of Heaven is like a camel getting through the eye of the needle?'

The reason is because Marx was stuck in his head, and if a person is stuck in their head they can only live in a world that can be identified and categorized, a materialistic world. Marx couldn't conceive of something beyond the visible world, because his mental cup was already full.

The purpose of religion is to remind us that we are not know-it-alls and that despite any structure society might create, we still have to have a heart. Faith is irrational because it is not in the head, it is in the heart. And there is no "design" for the future that will come out positive because designs come from the head, not the heart. Designs made by vanity are going to be vain, not positive.

*No problem can be solved from the same level
of consciousness that created it.*

– Albert Einstein

Are we going to bring a head trip without a heart on our journey to finding justice and beauty? Can we find beauty without questioning our own head trips?

The problem today, and always, is spiritual and the solution will be spiritual as we realign with what we really are deep inside : quiet, connected, caring, empathetic, and loving.

* * *

In this text before you, I will return again and again to phony, distracting, soul smearing sexuality and its relationship in allowing crime. Force dovetails with seduction, seduction dovetails with force. Stick and Carrot, Carrot and Stick. (I'm talking about leading a donkey, for those who don't get the metaphor.) The carrot is often seductive and hides the stick.

Sex can masquerade for love and hide the currents of hate. "Lipstick and war crimes" refers to this relationship of seduction and force, and how they work together. This will become more clear as we meet some of the characters in the story.

We can't solve one distortion without solving the other. We won't end war and still be phony mannequins. We will all have to get very real to face our responsibility to clean up the mess we are in. Though older people might be de-moralized, complacent and plump, and younger people utterly distracted, and everyone fairly intoxicated, I feel the economic crisis we are all facing will not be our common enemy, but our common friend in helping us get down to Earth and save the day.

However we will NOT do this under the thumb of the UN or Club of Rome, organized by the rich corrupt elite. We will do this by cutting them off and revitalizing our own communities and being self-regulating, as people have lived since ancient times.

It is not backwards to become sane again.

* * *

A policeman that I heard of, arrested someone with a car full of drugs. The next day a well dressed man was at the front door of his home and told him to back off on the arrest and offered him money. "You arrested my cousin yesterday. You have a family you know. Do you want silver or lead?" The policeman had no choice. He had a family.

What would have been the offer if a pretty young woman with boobs and legs and belly button hanging out had come to his door? What message would she have had? As we will learn, politics is run with beta-trained women arriving at the door. "Velvet or lead?" Most politicians don't need more money. But sex, now, hot, now? This is how our world is run. I know you don't believe it! You will meet some of these women in a few pages. It is fear of exposure that is the stick and illicit sex is often the carrot. The carrot in diplomatic circles often grotesquely includes pedophile child trafficking. (This carrot and stick is part of the Entertainment industry also. That is, you put out, or you don't get the contract.)

Another way to say it is that the White House and the UN are very much "in bed" with sexual deviancy as are international circles which meet at places like Bohemian Grove in northern California. [10] King Idris of Libya had international pedophile parties before he was ousted by hero Gaddafi. I met a woman whose father worked at the UN in New York and she said that the offices had secret passage bathrooms (for secret sex) built into them from the get go.

(A conspiracy is simply a secret organization. The largest secret organization in the world are the Freemasons whose symbolism has been used now by an evil group, referred to as the Illuminati by George Washington, as long ago as 1789. This group is part and parcel with the Banksters.)

* * *

If men and women were equal the ability to seduce and tempt wouldn't be possible, but we are not equal. Without some kind of internal mitigation, men go crazy without sex, so there is an insatiable need, at least in a society with little spiritual practice. A *dominant culture* like ours, that runs on forced extraction from the frontiers, doesn't give a damn about spiritual practice or "internal laws." So the Spanish conquistadors or the settlers of Australia or the American soldiers who invaded Vietnam or the Russians who overran Budapest or the Muslim Pakistani army that raped hundreds of thousands of Muslim Bangladesh women in 1971 [11] shows that without internal moral codes, many men can become animals.

Bangladesh 1971—"Thousands of Bengali women were abducted and held by force in barracks, where they were raped night after night for months … Author Susan Brownmiller relays the words of an Indian reporter who writes that *pornographic movies* were shown to soldiers 'in an obvious attempt to work the men up.'" [12] (That is, they were *socially engineered* to ignore the women's humanity and see them as just objects so they could act out immoral aggression. Our entertainment industry is doing this to us all now.)

It seems that human beings can swing toward compassion or abuse, and the length of the arc of the pendulum is based on spiritual guidance or it's opposite. How else do we explain restraint and excess?

Immoral sex is used in war to de-moralize the subjugated nation and emblazon the aggressors. The U.S. military is still hiding illicit sexual rituals. "… incidents of sexual assault increased 50 percent between 2012 and 2013 … men, who make up half of all reported victims of sexual assault, according to a Pentagon study released last week." [13]

Kill, rape, steal. Western culture is an empire culture built on endless war, which used to be called colonialism, but now is called trade agreements. "Globalization" is an empire culture as shown by the "austerity measures" of the IMF which use "law" to extract debt to feed banksters. The IMF economically rapes victim nations for the benefit of empire. [14]

An extracting culture is not a self-sufficient sustainable culture. It is predatory. Because ours is an extracting culture involved in lust for what other nations have, it should be no surprise that celibacy is dishonored. Since our culture is bent on ever more extraction in order to "progress" we can see that our progress is predatory. We believe in predatory progress.

This is difficult to express and I can see I'm having a hard time of it. I am saying that sexual restraint and the restraint of violence are related. Nuns and peace goes together. Lipstick and war crimes go together.

* * *

Many *indigenous men* practiced strict celibacy or strict monogamy. The Hopi of Arizona as described by author Frank Waters or the 20% of Old Tibet that were monks, are examples.

But where ever there are large concentrations of people in cities, the opportunity for deviance seems to expand. In anonymous urban life, it seems there is more temptation to experiment with the illicit, the immoral, the wrong.

As the Spanish crossed lake Texcoco in 1519 to enter Tenochtitlan, now known as Mexico City, they encountered some boats with prostitutes painted red. The paint made them less human, less recognizable as individuals with unique character and karma. But this was Toltec city life. Out in the bush, women didn't do this with the community that had known them since infancy. In unnatural settings like large cities or in extreme circumstances, sex has been a trade item. In other words, sex gets distorted when there are unnatural concentrations of people.

* * *

There are women who have put forth the idea of a patriarchal conspiracy. I don't think they are seeing that a lot of human behavior is a result of conditions, not intentions.

Women should know that it is the prostate gland that makes your husband (or husband to be) aroused each morning with a full bladder pressed against it. (So much for cosmetics, eh?) It is not his *intent* to get aroused. I think that the vast majority of people in world were created because of the prostate gland, not a decision to have a child. No one ever talks about this. I think that this mechanism may be a big part of human reproduction. If this is true, which it may or may not be, did a patriarchal conspiracy create the prostate gland and it's function? Women can bear children starting as young teens, but few boys that age have the skills to support a family. A natural age gap is seen in marriages world wide. This wasn't intentional. No patriarchy created this age gap. Go to any high school. Few girls are attracted to younger guys. Did patriarchy create this?

Arranged marriages were the norm across most cultures, so that young girls didn't have children without support. Girls become women by the age of 14. In extended families, the in-laws needed to get along. So marriages were arranged because it was two families getting married. This was the civilized way before the wrecking ball of modern *social engineering* steered us to infatuation and lust. Sex appeal means lust appeal. Falling in love these days is often falling in lust. Ancient societies knew this was a big mistake.

As the reader is about to see, feminism as we know it has gone through different phases, and the blame game against patriarchy was created to help destabilize all of us. Because girls come of age sooner than boys and husbands are older than wives, *patriarchy will never end because seniority will never end*. Kick and scream, what I just wrote is true forever. Seniority doesn't cause abuse, crime does. Crime comes with the absence of morals, de-moralization. An empire culture is not criminal because of men, it is criminal because of lack of morality.

* * *

The idea that women have to do something to be sexy is very odd. Who created this idea? Women don't have do anything to be sexy! Men love women because they don't look like men! But the Globalists do not want whole communities made of stable strong whole families where sexuality is channeled into wholesome good relationships. They don't want anything whole, holy or sacred. They want fragmentation and the profane. They want us de-moralized. That means without morals. They want women to dress for sex every day, and constantly be seeking sexual attention. (More in Vol. 2, Chapter 7) They want serial affairs, which leads to more broken homes with children who are easier prey for their social engineers.

This is why, if you are a woman, you spend time painting yourself to be "sexy." You were conditioned to do this. This is why you are a sex object now. A whole family is built on wholesomeness. The Globalists want to trash standards so they can have a clean slate to place their own standards. They want broken families that won't resist their designs. So they are very busy "transforming" innocence to licentiousness. You can see this in how movies, songs and TV has changed in just the last two decades, particularly since puppet agent Madonna (proof upcoming). They really want a virtue-free zone. This means they want a conscience-free zone. By doing this, people won't stand up for what is right, because they will have lost their compass and connection.

Today, all women in the "developed" countries are sexualized from an early age. That would be every woman the reader knows. We need to save ourselves from this programming and save *indigenous peoples* from this globalized virtue-free campaign. Yes, the *Lipstick and War Crimes* series is a call to action. If you are looking for a cause here it is. Save innocence everywhere!

  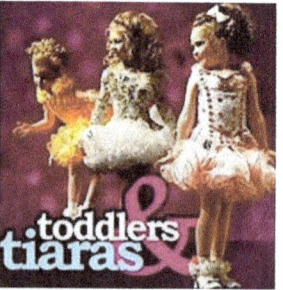

There is little difference between protecting innocence, and protecting the natural feminine. We need Mama Bear to stand up to this assault. We need all women and men to stand up and say "Leave our children alone!"

Some Female Icons of Globalist Social Engineering

Six central figures in our government's Feminist Operation have been Gloria Steinem, Marilyn Monroe, Katherine Hepburn, Madonna, Hillary Clinton, and Beyoncé Knowles. (I include some info about Shirley MacLaine, Angelina Jolie, and Miley Cyrus also.)

CIA Gloria Steinem

Lauded "Mother of Feminism" Gloria Steinem was a CIA agent and the CIA funded *Ms. Magazine*. What!

" ... In my view, her intelligence role in decimating the feminist movement was even more destructive. I (like Betty Friedan, who confronted her publicly at a national meeting) hold her personally responsible for the organizational chaos in the National Organization for Women that drove working class women out of the movement and caused the Equal Rights Amendment to fail.

"Less well known is another operation Steinem ran to plant so-called "black feminists" in grassroots African American groups to break them up (see http://rah.posterous.com/black-feminism-the-cia-and-gloria-steinem-fwd). I ran across some of these nasties in Seattle, while working to set up an African American Museum in the late eighties. I write about it in my recent memoir: *The Most Revolutionary Act: Memoir Of An American Refugee* (www.stuartbramhall.com). I currently live in exile in New Zealand."

– comment by Dr. Stuart Jeanne Bramhall, February 28, 2011

The following are points collected from various websites. [15]

- Gloria Steinem is a CIA Agent and everything she has ever done throughout her adult life has been under the direction of the CIA. Gloria Steinem was recruited into the CIA before she even graduated high school.

- Gloria Steinem, was from a poor and dysfunctional family and had almost no contact with her father. She lived in a house without running water, but was able to attend the elite and expensive Smith College. She received a "Chester Bowles Student Fellowship" to "study" in India. This was a Fellowship created by the CIA to cover Steinem's expenses in India—no one else has received a "Chester Bowles Student Fellowship" either before or since Steinem received it. In India she probably received massive programming, away from any former friends or family. In other words she was groomed and was never independent.

- One of Gloria Steinem's first missions for the CIA was to manipulate the student movement (most people are unaware that the National Student Association was created, funded and manipulated by the CIA). Steinem did this by organizing "student festivals" in Europe in the 1950s and 1960s. Steinem used the "student festivals" to spy on students for the CIA and she likely used the festivals to recruit new agents. A second and more successful mission was to *shift the orientation* of the "woman's movement" and splinter the Black Revolution of the 1960s.

- In 1958, Cord Meyer, head of the CIA's International Organizations division (IO), had a plan. The Agency would provide discreet funding to an "informal group of activists" who would constitute themselves as an alternative American delegation to the Vienna festival. The CIA would not only pay their way but also assist them to distribute books and publish a newspaper in Vienna. Among other individuals, Meyer and his colleagues hired Gloria Steinem to work with them. Steinem had recently returned from a two-year stint in India.

- Corroboration for her festival work comes from Kai Bird's book, *The Chairman: John J. McCloy and the Making of the American Establishment* (1992) (pp. 483-84, 727): "In the summer of 1959, just before McCloy took his family for an extended trip to Europe, C.D. Jackson wrote to remind McCloy that later that summer a World [Globalist] Youth Festival was scheduled to take place in Vienna. Jackson asked McCloy to contribute a propaganda article. The piece would appear in a daily newspaper to be published in Vienna in conjunction with the festival. McCloy agreed, and the article was published (in five languages) in a newspaper distributed by a twenty-five-year-old Smith graduate named Gloria Steinem."

- In 1958, Steinem was recruited by CIA's Cord Meyers to direct the "informal group of activists" called the "Independent Research Service." *That is, Steinem started the Independent Research Service.* This was part of Meyer's "Congress for Cultural Freedom [doublespeak for cultural homogenization and slavery]," which created magazines like "Encounter" and "Partisan Review" to promote a left-liberal chic to oppose Marxism. It was this operation that Steinem's "student festivals" was a part of. Besides spying on students, Steinem also acted as an agent provocateur, helping to provoke riots. While co-director, she wrote in 1959 an interesting pamphlet, *A Review of Negro Segregation in the United States*, in which she states that while *some* discrimination still exists, it is largely in the minds of the oppressed.

- However as a testament to the dishonest culture at Steinem's *Ms. Magazine*, in the 1997 book *Inside Ms.: 25 Years Of The Magazine And The Feminist Movement*, former *Ms. Magazine* editorial staff member Mary Thom claimed that the Independent Research Service entity "had been founded by former National Student Association officials"—not by Steinem; and that "Steinem learned of the CIA financing from National Student Association people."

- Commenting on the CIA-controlled "student festivals" organized by Gloria Steinem, Sheila Tobias, an unwitting participant on one such trip (who later taught women's studies at Cornell University), said the CIA: "was interested in spying on the American delegates to find out who in the United States was a Trotskyite or Communist. So we were a front, as it turned out." (quoted by Marcia Cohen in *The Sisterhood*, 1988)

- Also attending the 1962 Helsinki Youth Festival with Steinem under CIA sponsorship was Barney Frank, who subsequently became an aide to Democratic Boston Mayor Kevin White and then a long-time Massachusetts Democratic representative in Congress. As *The Pied Piper: Allard K. Lowenstein and the Liberal Dream* by Richard Cummings would note in 1985:

"Barney Frank at Harvard had been with the Independent Research Service delegation to Helsinki, an operation which, by Frank's own admission, he clearly understood was CIA-backed. Frank joked about the role of fellow delegate Gloria Steinem, whom he described as "running around at nightclubs set up by the CIA in Helsinki, helping to win over Africans."

This was her use of training as a sexual agent, which is what female CIA agents do. Lipstick and war crimes.

- Working through C.D. Jackson and Cord Meyer, Steinem set up an organization in Cambridge, Massachusetts called the "Independent Service for Information on the Vienna Youth Festival." She obtained tax-exempt status, and Jackson helped her raise contributions from various American corporations, including the American Express Company (alleged CIA connections). But most of the money came from the CIA, to be managed by

Jackson in a "special account." The entire operation cost in the range of $85,000, a considerable amount in those years. (Another source says $180,000)

- A CIA Operative named Samuel Walker, who made a career as president of Walker & Co. (a New York City publishing firm founded in the same year as the CIA funded Publications Development Corporation) evaluated Gloria Steinem's contribution to the CIA operations ...

  "Gloria's group continues to do yeoman service, distributing books etc. to the point where the cry has gone up 'Never before have so many Young Republicans distributed so much Socialist literature with such zeal." Walker praised Steinem's "female intuition" and wrote, "Gloria is all you said she was, and then some. She is operating on 16 synchronized cylinders and has charmed the natives ... "

  – C.D. Jackson to Cord Meyer, 7/14/59,
  with attached Walker diary; Walker to Jackson, 7/31/59, DDE.

In other words, Gloria Steinem was NOT a naive dupe of the CIA, as she and *Ms. Magazine* employees have let on. She was a highly motivated agent.

- When this covert operation was revealed by *Ramparts* magazine in 1967, CIA Gloria Steinem told *The New York Times* that she approved the Agency's role.

  "I was happy to find some liberals in government in those days who were farsighted and cared enough to get Americans of all political views to the Festival."

CIA Steinem's definition of a "liberal" then included such young men as Zbigniew Brzezinski, an assistant professor at Harvard. Steinem arranged to fund Brzezinski's visit to the "student festival." (Brzezinski would later become the National Security Advisor to President Jimmy Carter (1977-1981), help found Rockefeller's Trilateral Commission and help manipulate the Soviet Union into invading Afghanistan. Brzezinski also then organized and funded Osama Bin Laden's "Jihad" against the Soviets in Afghanistan. He wrote the *The Grand Chessboard: American Primacy And Its Geostrategic Imperatives* and some feel he was Obama's handler when Obama was supposedly studying at Columbia University.)

- CIA Gloria Steinem befriended Black writer Alice Walker and paid for Walker to come to the CIA-manipulated "student festival" in Vienna. Lesbian Alice Walker later became the foremost writer of anti-Black male hate books (according to some in the Black male community) — all of which were funded by money funneled to her publishers by the CIA. Her lesbian leaning book *The Color Purple* was made a movie by Illuminati controlled Hollywood (proof upcoming) as part of the de-moralization program. CIA Gloria Steinem has boasted in interviews with the *NY Times* and the *Washington Post* (in 1967) that her training with the CIA was "good journalistic training" because the CIA "taught you to be accurate." This statement proves that Steinem was happy to collect money working for the CIA and was conscious of what she was involved with.

In February 21, 1967 a *New York Times* article confirmed the *Ramparts Magazine* disclosure. CIA Steinem had told the *Times* that: (1) the CIA had been "a major source of funds" for the

Independent Research Service since its formation in 1958; (2) "she had talked to some former officers of the National Student Association, who told her CIA money might be available;" (3) she "was a full-time employee of the service" until 1962; and (4) "The CIA's big mistake was not supplanting itself with private funds fast enough." [Shell companies to fake the true source.]

- CIA Gloria Steinem worked with Carlos Bringier, the anti-Castro Cuban who staged the famous WDSU interview with Lee Harvey Oswald. She had very high top connections.

- CIA Gloria Steinem dated J. Stanley Pottinger *for nine years*. To some Black activists Pottinger was in charge of sabotaging civil rights enforcement at the Justice Department (he was assistant attorney general) under President Nixon and President Ford. According to Donald Freed & Fred Landis in their book *Death in Washington*, J. Stanley Pottinger helped to cover up the government assassinations of Martin Luther King and Chilean Orlando Letelier. (James Earl Ray was exonerated in Court in Shelby, Tennessee 1999 and the government was implicated in this censored-from-media and history books 30-day trial. James Earl Ray DID NOT KILL Martin Luther King. [16]) Pottinger publicly defended Gloria Steinem against charges of CIA involvement—*which Steinem had already admitted*. How did she meet Pottinger and why was she with him?

> "An Iranian banker in New York City who offered to help seek the release of the American hostages in Iran in 1980 is under investigation for leading a group that purportedly smuggled banned military equipment into Iran, according to federal authorities. The investigation, which began four years ago, resulted in the arrests in New York last month of the brother of the banker and of a Huntington, Long Island businessman on smuggling charges. According to federal officials, a former United States Assistant Attorney General, W. Stanley Pottinger, is also under investigation. The 44-year-old Mr. Pottinger, who was in charge of the Civil Rights Division in the Justice Department from 1973 to 1977, recently testified before the federal grand jury in Manhattan investigating the case. He did not return telephone calls left at his Manhattan office or his home."
>
> – by Solwyn Rab, *New York Times*, 6/3/1984

According to Gail Collins, Huffington Post, 3/25/2014, CIA Gloria Steinem "had been seeing" Henry Kissinger. Kissinger did his PhD thesis on the 1814 Illuminati Congress of Vienna and is an international war criminal, pedophile, child killer, member of the Bohemian Club and secret elite Bilderberg group leader. That is the short list. Why would a "liberal feminist" bed someone who was considered a mass murderer in the decimation of rural Laos and Cambodia [17] by everyone familiar with the Vietnam war?

In image compilation above, the symbol she is showing is the triangle with the *all-seeing-eye*, which I call the Pyramid of Abuse, which we will see many many times used by in-the-club celebrities. (Some feel it is a mind control diamond symbol.) "Moving into the future" at bottom left means the ONE future that the Globalists will dictate for EVERYONE. Gloria will be your female Big Brother. Brzezinski, center above. To right, younger Kissinger.

Kissinger was also responsible for the "premeditated, wholesale destruction of the environment using chemical defoliants such as Agent Orange," as Tatchell wrote in *The Guardian*. "These are war crimes under the 1957 Geneva Conventions Act." [18]

The fact that career CIA agent Gloria Steinem was "seeing" Henry Kissinger indicates that he was one of her handlers as part of her programming. Steinem is presently associated with Jane Fonda as co-founders of the Women's Media Center. Two peas in a pod? Why hasn't Fonda ever outed Steinem as a known CIA agent, if she is such a progressive activist? (How about Walker?)

How did Jane Fonda get actress positions? Everyone in Hollywood knows how young actresses are vetted. (See Shirley MacLaine, coming up soon.) Fonda's 1972 trip to Vietnam was probably a covert courier operation, similar to Cathy O'Brien's assignments in Central America. (We will meet hero whistleblower Cathy O'Brien shortly.) Fonda was married to Tom Hayden who to this day writes disinformation for the official story. That is, his writing appears to be alternative, but he doesn't include crucial details and so misleads his readers. (Page 73) Fonda then married billionaire globalist CNN Ted Turner, who among other things, was a friend and supporter of David Rockefeller, one of the most corrupt men in history. Who is Jane Fonda?

Jane Fonda, interestingly, like Steinem, comes from a dysfunctional family, from where children are often acquired to be programmed into multiple personalities in a process organized under Nazi research, later called MK-Ultra. Oprah Winfrey started getting raped when she was age nine [19] and Beyoncé Knowles was pregnant at age 14, despite living in a reported very controlled home. [20] Fonda, Steinem, Madonnna, MacLaine, Winfrey and Knowles are programmed agents from childhood. "My mother was actually abused as a child and killed herself when I was 12, and that is just for starters," Fonda told FOX 411's Pop Tarts column. Madonna, another agent, has a similar background without a mom. (Vol. 2, Chapter 8)

Now that the reader understands a wee wee bit about mind programming and early sexuality, and that most everything we have been told about CIA Steinem is a lie, do you really believe the following is the whole story ... "In 1963, Gloria Steinem worked as an undercover bunny for 17 days at Hugh Hefner's New York City Playboy Club." Steinem was already a CIA operative, so obviously she was placed. The CIA would not have allowed anything like this without their supervision. One would have to disregard the entire history presented above to believe that Steinem was a playboy bunny as part of some legitimate investigation as an independent journalist because, in fact, she was never independent. Like *Ms., Playboy* magazine is CIA. [21]

This was just a cover story, as was Jane Fonda's stunts in Vietnam. There is no way Jane Fonda could have betrayed POW's in her 1972 visit to Hanoi, and got away with it, if it was true. [22] There is no coincidence that Tom Hayden is now a disinformation agent and was also on that trip to Vietnam. Both Fonda and Hayden were and are agents. Founder CIA Steinem is now a board member of Women's Media Center, (with co-founder Fonda). That means the CIA controls the Women's Media Center, which both Hayden and Fonda are silent about, because they are agents also. Fonda starred in recent sexual blurring Netflix series, *Grace and Frankie.*

Gloria Steinem is stable in her programming. Receiving awards, as we see in image below, is part of the programming. That is, CIA Gloria Steinem actually *believes she is right and what she thinks should be applied to all other people world wide*. She actually believes this. She and others are given awards for thinking like this to build up the lie of their false ego. This is the disease of *disconnecting vanity*. As I will repeat several times in this writing, award ceremonies are all about sealing covert activity. This includes the Medal of Freedom award. It includes the VMA and Grammy Awards that celebrate puppets who don't write the songs, don't produce the choreography, and who simply obey day after day, year after year, in what some people feel is a hell which they rarely recover from. The award ceremonies create an acceptable closure for operations which are much more complex and undiscussed.

Fame is not the reward of talent or genius, as we are led to believe.

People like Steinem, Madonna, Fonda, Bill Clinton and Obama, who we are told rise from the dust, are in reality agents who were programmed very early. Seeing this pattern, Steinem was probably mind programmed, which involves sexual compromise, since before her teen years. Kissinger as we will learn, was a top pervert and programmer. "Seeing each other" certainly didn't mean that Kissinger and Steinem had an exclusive relationship. She spent time being programmed by him as an obedient slave, as did many others. She submitted her will to his will. This keeps her in the cage. We return to Kissinger in more graphic detail in *Lipstick and War Crimes: Vol. 3,* but you can speed ahead here [23].

Again, why was CIA Gloria Steinem in a loveless sexual relationship with a war criminal? And since that is very much the truth, what moral coordinates can she offer anyone about anything? Shouldn't we keep asking that?

Below we see CIA Gloria Steinem (the reader now understands that prefacing her name with "CIA" is not an epitaph, but an accurate title) receiving an award for her obedience from third generation CIA agent Obama. Yes, you read that correctly.

If the reader would like to speed ahead about Obama, read the book, *The Manufacturing of a President* by Wayne Mansen. The Black man in flower leis in below image is claimed to be Obama's biological father, Obama Sr. but this is very much disputed, even by members of his family in Kenya. [24] In photo below is a White guy with white shirt. That is Obama's mom's father, (Obama's grandfather) Stanley Armour Dunham, a "furniture" salesman who just happened to be at the airport to greet Obama Sr. personally. The young Kenyan, Obama Sr., was brought over in a CIA African student program to be trained in U.S for later placement as an operative. Obama's mom, Ann Dunham, who carried on in father Stanley Dunham's profession in the CIA, called herself an anthropologist. She helped in the military take over of Indonesia, in which over a million people were hunted down and killed. The role of this same Indonesian military will come up soon in discussion of the abuse toward *indigenous peoples*. Both parents of Obama are said to have died tragically. Again, both Obama's parents were CIA agents and both are claimed to have died in "accidents." In fact, they were both eliminated so as not to influence or expose, in any possible way, the CIA Manchurian candidate we know as Barack Hussein Obama. I know you don't believe it! Look at the photos on the next page, and allow your mind to register new evidence.

[VIDEO] Wayne Madsen Bombshell: Barack Obama ... - YouTube

www.youtube.com/watch?v=XEtHy0zuZT8

By The Alex Jones Channel · 15 min · 33,168 views · Added Aug 19, 2010

Bombshell: Barack Obama conclusively outed as CIA creation NEWS ALERT: Investigative journalist Wayne Madsen is scheduled to appear live on the Alex Jones ...

Wayne Madsen: Obama's CIA Connections, Part I and II ...

www.veteranstoday.com/2010/08/18/wayne-madsen-obamas-cia...

— Special Report: The Story of Obama: All in The Company Part I – By Wayne Madsen WMR [Wayne Madsen Report] has discovered CIA files that document the agency's ...

Wayne Madsen Bombshell Barack Obama Conclusively Outed ...

curlyhairstyles2015.com/pdkt/wayne-madsen-bombshell-barack-obama...

Curlyhairstyles2015.com give you info about Wayne Madsen Bombshell Barack Obama Conclusively Outed As and read our other article related to Wayne Madsen ...

Wayne Madsen Special Report – Obama and Emanuel: ...

atlah.org/2010/06/10/wayne-madsen-special-report-obama-and-emanuel...

Wayne Madsen Special Report – Obama and Emanuel: Members of Same Gay Bath House Club in Chicago. Posted on 10 June 2010. ... Subscribe to my YouTube ...

[PDF] Wayne Madsen Obama All in the Company

exopolitics.blogs.com/files/wayne-madsen-obama-all-in-the-company.pdf

In the second part of his investigation Wayne Madsen focuses on Barack Obama's mother and stepfather.

Obama's parents obviously did not meet in a Russian language class. Every single thing we ever heard about Obama was a fabrication, including this one from controlled Wikipedia. "1961: Dunham and Obama Sr. were married on the Hawaiian island of Maui on February 2, 1961, despite parental opposition from both families." What a lie, it was an arranged marriage, and that is why the loveless marriage, and the scheduled convenient divorce, was not contested by Obama Sr. who was a cover for Barack's real father, Frank Marshall Davis. See deeper discussion here. [25]

Photos below from Frank Marshall Davis's collection, show us that Ann Durham, Obama's mother, was not some innocent hippie anthropologist. This shows that she was involved with sexual beta kitten programming to destroy sexual inhibitions, as are most female agents. There is some evidence she was given to Davis at age 13. Like Shirley MacLaine, who we will meet shortly, Anne was given over to CIA programs by her CIA dad Stanley Dunham, for beta training to be described soon. Obama had a male nanny who was a transexual. This was a CIA selection to strip him of clear polarity. If one thinks there is no such thing as male and female, then there is no basis for up and down, in or out, or right and wrong either. If nothing is clear, everything is blurred.

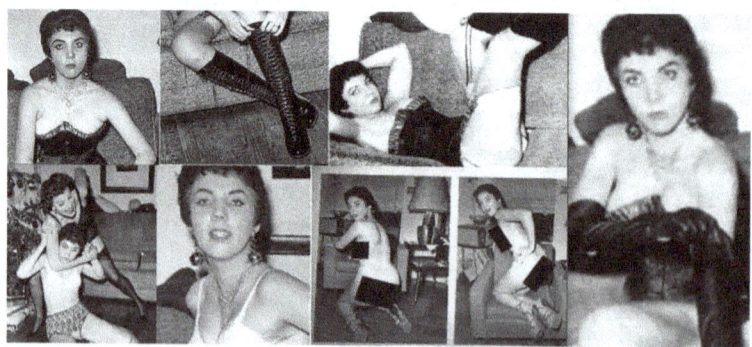

- One of the principle stockholders in CIA Gloria Steinem's *Ms. Magazine* was Catherine Graham. In the book *Catherine The Great* by Deborah Davis, the longstanding involvement of Graham's publishing empire (which includes *The Washington Post* and *Newsweek*) with the CIA was documented at considerable length. (Remember this fact when we cover Graham in Barbara Walters' selection of famous women at end of Vol. 1.)

- CIA Gloria Steinem *has lied often about her career and where she gets her money.* For example, she received money to start *Ms. Magazine* from the publisher of the racist *New York Daily News*, real estate magnate Mortimer Zuckerman. CIA Steinem lied to *Vanity Fair*, claiming that Zuckerman provided no money for *Ms. Magazine*. But columnist Liz Smith revealed that Zuckerman had put $1.2 million into *Ms. Magazine* and sent his executives to help as well. Steinem is a not a pathological liar, she is CIA.

- CIA Gloria Steinem's literary career was conceived and executed by people such as Clay Felker who wrote propaganda for the "Youth Festivals." In the early 1960s, he became an editor at *Esquire* and published articles by Steinem *which established her* as a leading voice for the CIA "Feminist Movement." In 1968, as publisher of *New York Magazine*, Felker hired Steinem as a contributing editor. Steinem was placed. Fame is created/placed.

- *Ms. Magazine*'s first publisher was Elizabeth Forsling Harris, a CIA-connected PR executive who planned John Kennedy's Dallas motorcade route. Despite its anti-establishment image, *Ms Magazine* attracted advertising from the cream of corporate America. It published ads for ITT (a CIA-supported corporation which helped engineer "Operation Chaos" in Chile, which led to the Kissinger directed CIA overthrow of a democratically elected government, and involved murder of thousands of people who believed in democracy. Warning, the next few sentences describe grotesque crimes against humanity.) "Amnesty International reports on what happened to women political prisoners under Pinochet's regime. 'One of the most grotesque things that I recall reading in the Amnesty International reports about the political repression and torture under Pinochet immediately after the overthrow of Salvador Allende in Chile, was that female political prisoners were often subjected to torture by specially trained dogs who would first rape them, and then sexually mutilate them.'" [26]

I'm sorry to shock the reader but *Ms. Magazine* is CIA and the CIA supported this kind of insane crime. Being feminine means two things … being soft and being Mama Bear, which means protecting the soft. We must protect the innocent. CIA *Ms. Magazine* does not. CIA is evil and *Ms. Magazine* will never criticize this evil because *Ms.* is CIA. Then, it is accurate and not exaggerated to say *Ms. Evil Magazine*.

Chile is now a globalist corporate farm where *indigenous peoples* have been reduced to the status of tenants. This is called "progress." This is why we should boycott imported fruits and vegetables and go local.

CIA Steinem actually "was seeing" the man who choreographed the coup against democratically elected Salvador Allende in Chile and he helped place monster dictator Pinochet. Kissinger denies this of course, but NOTHING he says can be trusted. More on that soon.

- When *N.Y. Times* reporters confronted CIA Steinem with documentation of her connections to the CIA and CIA funding of her various activities, Steinem remarked that she got caught because CIA wasn't tricky enough. Hinting that CIA should have made better use of front companies, Steinem remarked: "The CIA's big mistake was not supplanting itself with private funds fast enough."

  By the time Steinem founded *Ms. Magazine*, the CIA had learned how to funnel money through private individuals and shell corporations. *Ms. Magazine* was funded through private channels. Often the trail of funding for a covert operations now involves a string of private enterprises to deter tracking.

- In 1975, two important feminist leaders, Carol Hanisch and Kathie Sarachild, again accused Steinem of working for the CIA and directing the movement *toward moderation and capitulation*. Steinem ignored the accusations, hoping they would go away, but then noted feminist Betty Friedan implied that "a paralysis of leadership" in the movement "could be due to the CIA" and she demanded that Steinem respond. After three months, Steinem wrote a six-page letter to feminist publications describing her work with the CIA. "I naively thought then that the ultimate money source didn't matter" wrote Steinem, aiming to dispel the charge that she was still a government operative. As we read above she was not only an operative, she was a sexual operative giving much more than her naivete.

- An organization of white feminists called "Red Stockings" outed Gloria Steinem as a CIA agent. When Red Stockings tried to publish a book called *Feminist Revolution* in 1979 with a chapter that detailed Steinem's CIA connections, Steinem and her powerful CIA-connected friends forced Random House to delete the chapter on Steinem. Nevertheless the chapter appeared in the *Village Voice* on May 21, 1979, but only after the *Village Voice* had been threatened by Steinem's lawyers.

- Michele Wallace was "author" of *Black Macho And The Myth Of The Superwoman*, which was published in 1978. This book called Harriet Tubman and Sojourner Truth "ugly" and said they were poor role models because they were united with Black men. The book argued that Black women should turn their backs on Black men and "go it alone." The book contained a systematic attack on the Black male revolutionaries who led the Black Pride and Black Power movements of the 1960s. The book was touted by CIA Gloria Steinem as a book that would "change the agenda for years to come" and Steinem put it on the cover of her *Ms. Magazine*.

  "Steinem was accused of ghost writing *Black Macho* herself. The 25-year-old alleged author, Michele Wallace (who came out of nowhere), cracked under the public scrutiny, had a nervous breakdown, after which she went into hiding for over two years. Some suggest Wallace was likely a CIA-mind control victim and the two "lost years" were spent being re-programmed. (Re-hab) Later, Wallace would re-surface as a college professor—working the minds of the young Black women. Since then, the CIA's *Black Macho* book became the bible of Black feminism. [Black women] have been played like fiddles since *Black Macho's* publication in 1978 and have yet to regain control of their own minds or their own agendas. The CIA's BLACK MACHO operation was considered one of their most successful campaigns against the Black community. That is, until the CIA launched it's Crack Cocaine Operation against the Black community several years after." [27]

- Steinem was "on the agency's payroll" for 4 years, according to *America's Other Voice: The Story of Radio Free Europe and Radio Liberty* by Sig Mickelson. And in late February 1967, the then-32-year-old Gloria Steinem had told *Newsweek* magazine:

> *"In the CIA, I finally found a group of people who understood how important it was to represent the diversity of our government's ideas at the Communist festivals. If I had the choice, I would do it again."*

Pure doublespeak. The CIA is devoted to creating mono-culture under the banksters' pyramid of abuse. And so is Steinem-ized feminism, where an elite clique tries to define the culture for all women world wide. There is no such thing as "all women." Like the word "humanity," this is a label that reduces all diversity to one target. No one has the right to guide all women or all humanity. Ask any indigenous person.

The excerpt below succinctly summarizes the above information. The word "whore" is not slander in this case.

Meet Gloria Steinem, CIA Whore *from American Chronicle*

"Around 1968 she came under the wing of Clay Felker who was variously editor at Esquire, publisher of New York Magazine, and owner of the Village Voice. He provided some of the start-up money for Ms. magazine's preview edition of January 1972, but his interest in Steinem was not all of a sudden. The two had met at the Helsinki Youth Festival where Felker published the CIA propaganda and she oversaw disruption of the communist activities while seducing the kids into the American orbit and writing dossiers on them for the CIA.

"In addition to Felker's relatively modest contributions, Ms. received heavy support from Katherine Graham's *Washington Post* as well as from Warner Communications, Inc. *Newsweek* was an early and enthusiastic supporter of the Independent Research Service and of Steinem. But Katherine Graham's and editor Ben Bradlee's CIA roots ran deep and broad.

"Ms was noted for its pro corporate stance, taking in advertising from such CIA stalwarts as ITT, the firm famously associated with the bloody coup in Chile in 1973. It is also worth noting that she dated Henry Kissinger who was perhaps [not perhaps] the power behind the coup which brutally removed the democratically elected Salvador Allende.

"But that is not all of Steinem's CIA associations. She dated for many years Washington attorney Stanley Pottinger who was Assistant Attorney General for Civil Rights from 1973-77 under Nixon and Ford. Pottinger worked overtime to prevent any investigation into the Martin Luther King assassination when it became clear that evidence implicated the FBI in the crime, a fact which we explore in detail in other blog postings.

"While busily burying investigations into the King murder, Pottinger was working feverishly to cover-up the CIA's murder of Chile's envoy to the United States, Orlando Letelier who was a strong critic of the brutal right winged Chilean government established by the CIA. This affair, about which we previously reported, was sponsored by James and William Buckley.

"Later Pottinger would come under investigation for smuggling arms into Iran, an activity which placed him squarely in the CIA orbit.

"If these CIA associations were not enough, then we should move on to Elisabeth Forsling Harris who was *Ms's* first publisher. Sherman Skolnick reports that she, along with Jack Pewterbaugh at the Saul Bloom Advertising Agency, was heavily involved in planning the motorcade of President John Kennedy when he visited Dallas on November 22, 1963, and places her firmly among the murderers who conspired to overthrow the U.S. government.

"Now it is understandable why Steinem and Felker were ruthless in suppressing any publications which mentioned her association with the Agency as they did around 1975 when Random House was about to publish a book by The Red Stockings titled the *Feminist Revolution* which contained chapters about Steinem's CIA associations.

"Steinem, Felker, and Ford Foundation president Franklin Thomas, all threatened to sue Random House for libel if they published the chapters on Steinem's CIA activities. They applied the same pressure to the *Village Voice* which also produced a series on her domestic espionage activities."

– from American Chronicle, August 18, 2013

On CIA Steinem's website you will find this quote ...

> "Without leaps of imagination, or dreaming, we lose the excitement of possibilities. Dreaming, after all, is a form of planning."
>
> – CIA Gloria Steinem

What she is talking about is designing the future of everyone else as a Globalist. You see, Steinem and other feminists who have "found their voice" like to speak for ALL women. Therefore, "possibilities" means *social engineering* from on top. An all-seeing-eye. "One singular possibility for everyone," is what she means. And that is what the pyramid symbol with the hand means above.

For Globalists, the purpose of life is not service and nurturing and being part of a reciprocal circle. The purpose is to be king of the mountain, and experience the personal titillation, the "excitement" to change what has always worked in the past. If one is into exercising one's will for "fun," the playing field to game is the ancient. "Progress" is a contest, a game against what has already existed. "Progress" is a disregard for what is ancient in favor of what is "exciting."

The rapidity, the speed to alter that which has always worked, is the measure of "progress." Not quality, but speed. The faster the change, the more exciting for those seeking power with this kind of manipulation. The excitement is in the mind, however the innocent and the ancient is destroyed. I call this loser-creation, the creation of losers at the expense of the "excited" mind, excited with it's own vanity and "power." At the top of modern society, the richest most powerful people, as we will learn, are rapists and killers who select the most beautiful little children for their sacrifices. (I understand this is difficult to believe.) This is "exciting." I thought words like "demonic" were sensationalist hysteria until I studied it.

This **"excitement"** has become a mental value system for almost everyone.

We worship progress, we spit on the ancient. The bottom strata of every modern country now are the *indigenous people*. The vanity of "excitement" rejects those who don't play the game. And in crushing them is this sense of "power." Vanity needs trophies after all, as we see in this selfie to right by Indonesian military with a murdered local man.

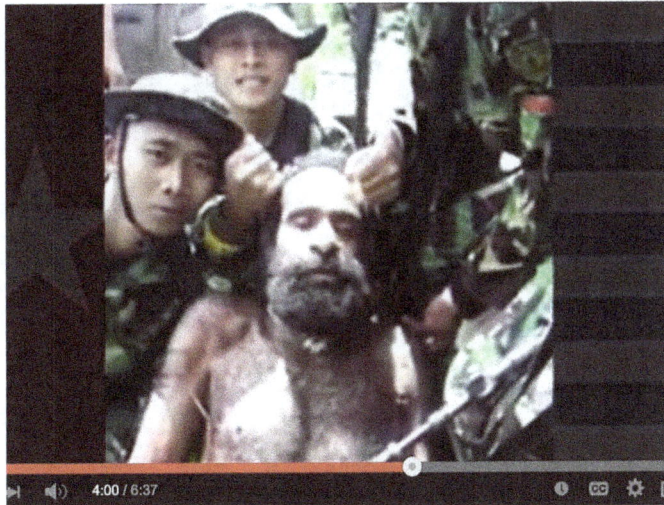

Presently, as of this writing, genocide is occurring in Papua New Guinea with U.S. backing. Over 700,000 locals have been killed for no reason. They will all be killed if we don't wake up to our role in destroying the ancient. Yes, this is horrible, and yes, our tax dollars are paying for this, as it is U.S. that originally trained and now props up the Indonesian military. [28] (Remember, Obama's mom helped install CIA Indonesian government.) This is why we cannot close our eyes. We must stop this. And we must change our values that think it is acceptable to destroy old traditions.

As in the trumped up Australian 2007 "Intervention," which invaded aboriginal reserves in Northern Territory, incidence of domestic violence in Papua is trumpeted by Western press while the real perpetrators, the Western regimes who destablized the ancient culture, are not mentioned.

Grasberg mine in Papua New Guinea is one of biggest gold/ copper/ silver mines in the world. On the Board of directors of Freeport-McMoRan Inc that owns the mine, are none other than Henry Kissinger and Gerald Ford, both pedophiles that used Cathy O'Brien (who we will meet shortly.) When the CIA is on a board of directors, it means the company is controlled by the CIA. It always means that. Kissinger is also a top Bilderberger, introduced in Chapter 3 of Vol. 2. The CIA is the power behind the Indonesian military, 40 years ago and now. "Sir" Henry Kissinger. This CIA puppet government is murdering the natives of Papua New Guinea, today, with your money.

You are the bottom of *their* pyramid and the top players are parasites that feed off of your sweat, and pay us all off with consumer items stolen from other lands. To be able to pay us off, the public must be turned from moral considerations, to sensual considerations. And that is what we see. We hold up the pyramid based on our ration of candy. Meanwhile, our taxes support the Indonesian government. We must stop this.

I don't think I could live without hair, makeup and styling, let alone be the performer I am. I am a glamour girl through and through. I believe in the glamorous life and I live one.

Lipstick and War Crimes (Lady Gaga)

Grasberg mine controversy

Main article: Grasberg mine

Freeport mines the world's largest gold reserve in the New Guinea Grasberg mine. In 2005, *The New York Times* reported that Freeport paid local military and police generals, colonels, majors and captains, and military units, in total nearly US$20 million between 1998 and 2004. One individual received up to US$150,000. The payments were meant to secure the reserve. Freeport responded that the payments were not for individuals, but rather for infrastructure, food, housing, fuel, travel, vehicle repairs and allowances to cover incidental and administrative costs. *The Times'* anonymous sources within the company also claimed that company chairman James R. Moffet courted Indonesia's dictator and "his cronies", cutting them in on deals. Another employee is said to have worked on a program to monitor environmentalists' e-mails and telephone conversations, in cooperation with Indonesian military intelligence officers.[22]

Freeport-McMoRan

From Wikipedia, the free encyclopedia

On October 17, 2011 the company halted operations in Papua amid a strike that led to a deteriorating security situation and intensified calls for Papuan independence. Seventy percent of Grasberg workers joined the strike, appealing for higher pay September 15, 2011, blocking roads, clashing with police and cutting the pipeline in several places.[23]

Citing extensive, long-term and irreversible environmental damage in New Guinea, The Government Pension Fund of Norway excluded Freeport-McMoRan from its investment portfolio, following a recommendation from the fund's ethical council.[24] **To "secure" the mine against the ancient locals so city people can have gold.**

Note on below: James J Stillman (1850-1918) Chairman of the Rothschild National City Bank, had daughters Elsie who married William Goodsell Rockefeller and Isabel who married his brother, Percy Avery Rockefeller. (Both Yale educated and members of Skull and Bones. Yale was created with Rothschild drug money. Mao was Dean at Yale China.) This intermarriage created "the Roth-fellers." National City Bank is now called CitiBank and is still Rothschild controlled as is Goldman Sachs Inc. Elsie's son Godfrey Stillman Rockefeller would help bring indigenous destruction and pollution world wide as a globalist, as seen below.

In 1935 the Board of Directors included chairman John Hay Whitney, Kidder, Peabody & Co., Eugene L. Norton, Langbourne M. Williams Jr. (president), Monro B. Lanier, Chauncey Stillman, Godfrey Stillman Rockefeller, David M. Goodrich. The company name was changed to Freeport Sulphur in December 1936.

Other directors included Augustus Long, Robert A. Lovett, Charles Wight from 1947, Benno Schmidt 1954-1997, Jean Mauzé, Robert W. Bruce III, Robert C. Hills, Paul W. Douglas 1981-1983 after serving on Freeport Minerals 1975-1981, Henry Kissinger 1988-1995, George Putnam, Mikhael Yosia and J. Taylor Wharton.

As of 2013, the board members are James R. Moffett, Richard C. Adkerson, Robert Allison Jr., Robert A. Day, Gerald J. Ford, H. Devon Graham Jr., Charles C. Krulak, Bobby Lee Lackey, Jon C. Madonna, Dustan E. McCoy, B. M. Rankin Jr. and Stephen Siegele.[26]

According to a study by Project Censored, "These men represent a portion of the global 1% who not only control the largest gold and copper mining company in the world, but who are also interconnected by board membership with over two dozen major multinational corporations, banks, foundations, military and policy groups. This 12-member board is a tight network of individuals who are interlocked with — and influence the policies of — other major companies controlling about $200 billion in annual revenues."[27][unreliable source?]

On December 28, 2015, it was announced that James R. Moffett would step down as chairman of the company.[28] Moffett will be replaced as chairman by Gerald J. Ford. It was reported that Moffett will earn a severance package that could total up

To "secure" the mine against the ancient locals so city people can have gold.

Do we see *Ms. CIA Magazine* or CIA Gloria Steinem defend *indigenous people* or criticize the CIA? Just as Fonda never criticizes Steinem, Steinem never questions Kissinger. Gloria Steinem is a change agent who spreads the "excitement" of feeling powerful and influential. So too is pop star Madonna, who also had CIA handlers. The same holds true for all the entertainment "Divas" we know today. This "excitement", as I said, must use something else to prove it is real. What does the mind find to prove it's own self importance? To prove it's own substantiability, *disconnecting vanity* (Glossary, Vol. 2) must change something else that is real and measure the rate of change. That something is the natural world, natural people, and natural women, which in this series, is called the *natural feminine*. The natural woman and natural man are the victims of vain "excitement." Vanity is parasitic on the natural and the ancient. And our "progress" is all about vanity.

Steinem actually wants to re-write human nature, and in doing so we are impacting nature like never before. It is worse than unsustainable, it is criminal. To prove one has an "imagination," something has to be altered. *Disconnecting vanity* (the vanity that disconnects) must "transform" something. The faster the transformation, the more "exciting."

Ultimately every natural system and every natural culture is slated for destruction by globalist thinkers who want to design the future for "everyone." "Our future" means their design. The future of "progress" under the disconnected present power structure is that nature will be replaced by a mowed lawn, and we are blades of grass in that lawn.

The purpose of CIA agent Steinem's *Ms. Magazine* was to destroy traditional role models in order to fragment ancient understanding of male and female. It is just the way Mao's cultural revolution was waged in the West. We have to be "liberated" so that we can rigidly conform to a new expectation that is "politically correct." If we don't, then we are derided. The new jail is established with smear.

Feminism Was Created To Destabilize Society, Tax Women and set up the NWO
by TomLeykis1
87,732 views

In this youtube, above, it is revealed that the Rockefellers admit to having funded feminism, probably very early, to 1) be able to get women working and taxed, and 2) so that women are no longer watching children. This allows the State to influence children at an earlier age to create their "docile" slaves, so that the children come to see school and the State as their providing family and source of guidance, instead of the parents. (Now many school children receive two meals a day from the State, rather than their mom.)

To get women working, the imaginative, "excited" planners had to convince women that joining the rat race was being "equal."

The carrot to lead the donkey would be consumer items (which I call candy) such as cosmetics and clothing, which the new workers would buy in order to feed their new vanity. The carrot is not the things, but the new vanity. Placed actresses such as Katherine Hepburn would be used like puppets to create this new mold of how a woman should think of herself. (Placed puppets would be used as actresses, placed actresses would be used as puppets. Let's please understand that actor means puppet.) If we look at elementary school age girls 50 years ago, they were not sexualized. Now they are. How did this happen?

The documented facts above, that feminism was hijacked by a placed and funded CIA agent who brushed these continuing associations under the carpet for 50 years, and was not outed by "activist" Jane Fonda but was protected, should be very disturbing to anyone who respected CIA Steinem or anyone who wants to "empower women." You probably made key decisions in your life because of her false guidance. Or perhaps your mother and grandmother did. I myself, as a young man in the 70s, was influenced to be chivalrous and kiss a—to feminism. We were all suckered. We were socially engineered. We drank the kool aid. We thought feminism was noble.

CIA Gloria Steinem was and is another puppet. People are not allowed off the hook with the CIA. She stayed under their umbrella, and is given grand awards to bolster her false identity. She did whatever she was told to do and still does.

She gave us aberrant ideas and standards that have made three generations of women dysfunctional. If you are a woman, she took you away from the ancient *natural feminine,* and if you are a man she gave you a population of women disconnected from their feminine side. A false meme is in the heads of women world wide. "Equality" means homogenization by becoming more male and not being womanly anymore. It does not mean anything noble, fair, or even workable.

The pyramid symbol shows to those who are already slaves in the Illuminati club that Steinem is also enslaved. The message is, "See, we got her too." This reinforces the sense that members can't escape. It is a message of membership and a terrifying message, because "breaking flock," as sung in the 2012 Grammies (Vol. 2, Chapter 8) can mean death. All CIA agents know they are expendable. To be an intelligence agent is to lobotomize one's conscience willingly.

In CIA double speak, words mean the opposite of the dictionary meaning. "Reporting" means pushing an agenda with social engineering, "Rebelling" means destroying traditions that worked for ages, and "Truth-Telling" means lying. "Moving into the future" means the Globalist's dream as spoken by John D Rockefeller in 1906.

American Idol 2014 • Season 13 Episode 32 • Top 5

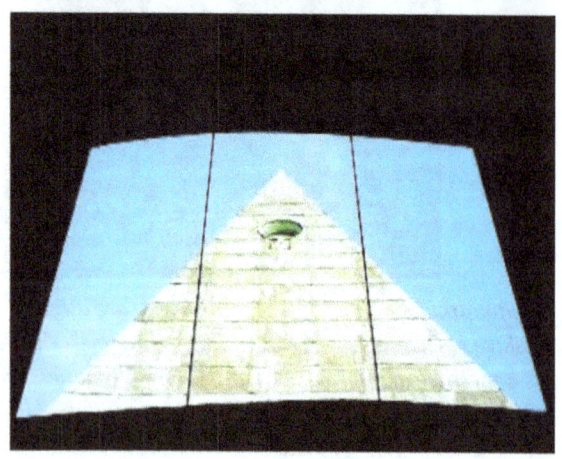

Steinem's pyramid hands are a symbol for the Illuminati pyramid and all-seeing-eye. Above, 1) all-seeing-eye on American Idol talent show staging, 2) subliminal eye in movie with young Disney brat Demi Lovato, 3) pyramid of abuse on jacket of agent Madonna, 4) Jay-Z seen also below, but above with eye, so make no mistake now what it means, which is not what concert audience is told in below image, 5) logo for DARPA, 6) and pyramid with all-seeing-eye on top of roof of the Dorothy Rothschild constructed Supreme Court Building in Israel.

I had heard of Steinem's name, but the first time I really wondered about her was when I was watching some market news on TV about fifteen years ago, when I was into that stupid stock trading gambling, and I saw a TV commercial by a financial institution which had a mock image of her name carved into a granite wall. Why this banking corporation was spending a lot of money spreading her name carved in stone was a puzzle to me. Later I realized the banks were plugging *Ms. CIA Magazine*, the foremost "voice" of hijacked feminism. The same people who control the banks through the FED, control the CIA, who control *social engineering*. This will become more clear in Vol. 2. We will see that pyramid symbol of Steinem's hands everywhere and analyze it. Below, insider Warren Buffet wants to reduce taxes for the rich, and that is fine with "Commander" Gloria Steinem. (See image text)

It's strange to fathom Chelsea Handler, Gloria Steinem, and Warren Buffett collaborating to reform America's tax code. But at the recent *Fortune* Most Powerful Women Summit, the edgy late-night talk-show host, the feminist icon, and the famed investor united around the "Buffett Rule," his proposal to lift taxes on the super-rich and equalize tax rates across classes. "I couldn't be more pleased," says Buffett, clearly pumped about his new supporters. "If I can get Chelsea and Gloria to command an army, I don't need more commanders."

It is only strange that they are collaborating, to those that think any of these puppets are independent. They are not. Warren Buffet funds the Gates Foundation. The Gates Foundation attempts to further the Rockefeller eugenist plan of top/down population control. The Rockefellers were funded by the Rothschilds. The Rothschilds are the banksters who ran the British Empire and now manage all of us, the BOP, the bottom of the pyramid, through THEIR global central bank system.

Ms. Lonely

"Ms." means "I am independent of a team called marriage" and thus "Ms." means a contractual association, not a surrender to union. Rather than ask men to also have titles that might denote marital status, women who use "Ms." want to be liberated and free like men. "Mrs." says to other men, "Hands off." Miss means available. Since it is the male who usually initiates courtship in the natural mammal world which we are a part of, the designations of Miss and Mrs. help sort out who is available and who is already married. The idea that women would give up this firewall is an invitation to temptation and trouble. Do "Ms." women wear wedding bands?

In CIA *Ms. Magazine* we behold centerfolds of naked men, because a "liberated" woman should act "equal" to chauvinist, lust driven men and see people as meat. This is CIA *Ms. Magazine* with no apologies. Carnal. The CIA is working for the banksters who want a craven lustful population that is bereft of the inner strength that comes from practicing virtue.

If you put on your indigenous eyes, this CIA *Ms. Magazine* centerfold is simply weird. Remember that most women reading *Ms.* are married or in a relationship, but *Ms. Magazine* didn't care about that. Quite the opposite.

The CIA produced this. Please keep remembering that. Not some ambitious women. This is the CIA. This is the CIA trying to change peoples' values toward the carnal and away from purity or refinement. Crude, gutter, low.

CIA 'Second Wave' feminism has been a race to the moral bottom, as we will see with Beyoncé in a few pages. The name of Steinem's copy-the-chauvinists magazine was a direct effort to fragment family loyalty using the ramped up and arrogant vanity of "liberated" professional women. The Globalists, through CIA funding, wanted to re-define the feminine to no longer include being feminine. If you look around, they are succeeding.

> Myrna Blyth was the editor in chief of "Ladies Home Journal" from 1981 to 2002. In her book, *Spin Sisters (2004)*, she says the media sold women "a career in exactly the same drum banging way that the Happy Homemaker had been sold to their mothers." (page 38 of her book)

The Illuminati undermined women's natural loving instincts using the following mantras:

1. "Men can no longer be trusted." Using the "Lifetime Network" as an example, Blyth concluded "all men are 1) unfaithful rats 2) abusive monsters 3) dishonest scumbags, or 4) all of the above. Women on the other hand were … uber-victims [or] flinty achievers who triumph despite the cavemen who … want to keep them in their place." (pages 62-63)

2. "Women are victims by virtue of their sex." Blyth says the media sends "one message loud and clear. Because we are women, we remain victims in our private lives, at work, in society as a whole." (page 156) Thus women must have a sense of grievance, entitlement and rebellion.

3. "Women should be selfish." "Liberation and narcissism have merged," Blyth says. Leisure now means, "time for yourself, spent alone, or perhaps with one's girlfriends but definitely without spouse and kids ... Endless articles preached the new feminist gospel, that indulging yourself is an important part of being a healthy, well adjusted woman." (page 65)

4. "Sex is not reserved for love and marriage." Magazines like *Glamour* and *Cosmopolitan* [Globalist owned] urge young women to "put out on their first date," "ogle men openly" and be an athlete in bed. There is no discussion of marriage or family. (page 160) Such women will not be able to trust any man enough to surrender themselves.

5. "Self-fulfillment lies in career success and not husband and family." "The social rewards of holding down a job are critical to one's sense of dignity and self worth," Betty Friedan pontificated. In fact, "most work is deeply ordinary," Blyth observes (pages 35-36).

"Thus many women are schizophrenic as they attempt to reconcile their natural instincts with a constant exhortation to do the opposite. The wreckage—broken families and dysfunctional people—is strewn everywhere.

"At the same time, *Playboy Magazine* etc. aimed a similar message at men. You don't need to get married to have sex. Marriage and children are a bore."

– Henry Makow [29]

Thus we see how the values of the people who now make up the illicit online sex clubs were steered into being. These values are not natural. CIA *Ms. Magazine* was at the fore front of this "exciting" imaginative campaign to produce a carnal illicit population.

"The narratives in our heads are not ours." – Debbie Lee

The "Humanitarian Intervention" Head Fake

Steinem helped the CIA hijack original and justice oriented feminism. A psy-op will be 95% true, so her (the CIA's) books at first focused on original feminist abuse issues. But as we already read in the quotes above by women's rights activists at that time, Steinem came to disrupt, and replace real feminism. A real feminist wants respect, not homogenization.

In my opinion, real abuse issues are well summarized by this song by Freddie Perren and Dino Fekaris, made famous by another Gloria, Gloria Gaynor.

First I was afraid, I was petrified, kept thinking I could never live without you be my side

But then I spent so many nights thinking how you did me wrong, and I grew strong, and I learned how to get along.

And so you're back, from outer space.

I just walked in to find you here with that sad look upon your face.

I should have changed that stupid lock, I should have made you leave your keys, if I had known for just one second you'd be back to bother me!

Go on now go! Walk out the door!

Just turn around now, cause you're not welcome anymore!

Weren't you the one who tried to hurt me with goodbye?

Did I crumble, did I lay down and die?

Oh no, not I. I will survive!

*Oh **as long as I know how to love** I know I'll be alive*

*I've got all my life to live and got **all my love to give**, and I'll survive!*

I will survive! Hey hey!

*It took all the strength I had, not to fall apart, and trying hard **to mend** the pieces of my broken heart*

And I spent oh so many nights just feeling sorry for myself, I used to cry,

but now I hold my head up high.

And you see me, somebody new!

I'm not that chained up little person still in love with you.

*And so you felt like dropping in and just expect me to be free! **Now I'm saving all my loving for someone who's loving me!***

Often what is true in one place is true somewhere else or is true in a bigger picture or different context.

The song above *identifies crime in general*, the reaction to crime, then renewal, and rebirth. The song does not demonize ALL men as being wrong in some way, or that boys should be drugged into submission so they will sit in class. The song does not call for a re-design of nature.

We need to raise boys like we raise girls.

–CIA Gloria Steinem

The song above proclaims that truth can win and the singer *is waiting for a better reciprocal relationship*. This is exactly what all independent cultures everywhere on Earth must do. We must throw out the Globalists, and return to community interaction which is local, reciprocal and not controlled from afar.

The original feminists were humanitarians lifting their voices against abuse. It was also noted at the time, that they were as a group, homely, and some joked they had never kissed a man. As outcasts, they wanted "equality" because they didn't fit into the polarity mold well. Their grievances were co-opted into a blame game to take down the head of the family, and when you do that, what is left is no family. Many Disney films (Walt Disney was also a placed puppet, Vol. 2, Chapter 8) featured a new theme. The new theme was the super heroine in movie after movie, particularly those aimed at the young through animation. I just watched an old 1948 movie and in it, the woman holds back, holds back, and then passionately leads in kissing the man. This was what we can call "the Lust Operation." *Ms. Magazine*, being CIA, is all about lust.

Many people criticize the seemingly passive women in early cartoons. The problem for the social engineers was that movies like *Cinderella* and *Snow White* still had a strong male in the story. Strong men might resist tyranny. Strong men supported by strong women in a strong family would especially resist tyranny. So this constellation was replaced in the minds of children with the super woman who never would have children, but dressed like a whore and was always "on." She is surrounded by weak stupid men. Both the male and female ideal would be undermined, and also parents in general would be ridiculed as incompetent and not worthy of respect. The sassy promiscuous female role model was born. The kids got Wonder Woman (Vol. 2, Chapter 7), the adults got *Ms. Magazine*.

"Woman on top" became a campaign. As I have a young daughter, she and I have seen many Disney and Pixar films and I'm amazed that 100% of the kiss scenes, not 98%, but 100% of the time, the girl makes the move. In the animated movie *Rio*, my daughter's favorite (she is older now), the female parrot is the new stereotype smart female. The male is the new stereotype passive clumsy fumbling "dumb blond." In *Rio*, the female parrot leads the kiss and in another scene jumps the boy parrot!

Every single movie is this way, and sure enough, at a music venue in Bolivia, I watched a young woman make the move so she could take a stranger home, all this in front of friends. Predatory promiscuity is now a women's prerogative, and modesty is long gone for many girls. The reader can say, "What is wrong with that? (Can't women be wanton also?)" What is wrong is love is based on love, not on lust. Love takes time and getting to know someone. Everything about it is wrong. I no longer let my daughter watch a movie unless I have seen it first. The only Disney cartoon movie I really like is the animated movie about horses called *Spirit*.

* * *

From a website definition of feminism …

"The basic assumption shared by feminists is that the gender of divisions in society [there are thousands of cultures in world, but globalists boil this down to "society"] operate to the disadvantage of women. [If one thinks men have some advantage in competing as slaves in a rat race.]

"The *process of gender socialization* [As with Rothschild employee Karl Marx, feminists think there are no organic or spiritual foundations for anything] usually encourages traditional [that's bad?] gender roles which reinforce and justify male dominance.

[Dominance, or specialization? What kind of dominance? Are men dominate in breast feeding? This question is never asked by rat race feminists. The blindness to ignore such an obvious question is the intentional blindness foisted by the social engineers. What we have is the co-option of everything feminine so that the only thing worthwhile is *to try to be a dominant manipulator.* What they mean is force. Yes, men are best at force, and women are best in the ways they dominate without force, and these are divergent spheres, as men and women rarely work together.]

"Feminists have shown that the so called [?] natural differences between men and women are not true. [The reader can go to any kindergarten class and observe.] Women are perfectly capable of building as successful a career as men are.

[Oh, so that is the final measure of equality! Getting a rat race slave job clawing up the ladder of status seeking and consumerism and getting two weeks of vacation per year! According to this definition of feminism, nature has been reduced to employability working for the unnatural machine which is killing the planet.]

"[CIA] Feminists have helped *transform* [key word – always take note when you see it] many of our assumptions [a million years of experience]. Women no longer feel their only goal in life is marriage and children.

[Does the reader see how it said "Women" meaning ALL women. Did "women" move on to something better … the goal to be entitled super consumers and ambitious wannabe egos in the "developed" "transformed" countries that crush and exploit other countries? Feminists get their equal turn with men at the deep and wide unsustainable pig trough called "progress." We need to see that the Western concept of freedom is based on us being rich at the expense of other peoples who we have stripped of their rights and land, to extract whatever we want, so we have "free time" to consume, travel, fantasize, and be "awesome."]

"In 1976 Sharpe interviewed girls regarding their aspirations in life. They put love and marriage as their top priorities in life with a career at the bottom.

"In 1996, she found that job and career were top of the list for girls, with marriage and children at the bottom." [30]

Perhaps, when enough women are "liberated," state run nurseries and boarding schools will be what *socially engineered* "liberated women" will want for their kids, since nourishing children will be seen as "the bottom of the list." And why get pregnant and miss work? Why not just have test tube/incubator babies so our careers can come first!

What happened in 20 years? Was it magic? How incredible that this apologist "learning" website for rat race feminism *didn't ask how* those values switched in just twenty years.

In fact an entire generation was "transformed" by a very organized program which we will be studying, not only in the media, but in our curriculums.

Law schools filled up with young women who put career before marriage, and then paid the price, when men their age could partner with younger, more attractive women and did. The *socially engineered* career girls, of course, blamed the men for knowing what is attractive. These successful she-rats in the rat race had no empathy for the young women who scored a more mature man. This is the disconnected ego, separated from nature, oblivious, clueless, arrogant and in denial of how reality works. In this series this is called *disconnecting vanity.*

Ancillary to trying to be superior is trying to stay superior, so wannabe-men not only want to be like lust driven men, but they want to look young forever. We will cover Elizabeth Taylor soon. Trying to paint youth onto one's face is a denial of the circle of life, which then deprives these women the chance to experience *being free of appearances as clear elders*. They are too busy trying, hopelessly, pathetically, to compete with young women.

All women who wear make-up are supporting the idea that men are superior, because men look okay enough already, without having to wear makeup, but women must become masked dolls to be "women," similar to the young women painted red in Mexico 500 years ago. Then being a "feminist" who wears makeup is rather contradictory if liberation is the desire. Such women are wearing double false pride. The woman is proud of wearing paint, and proud she is equal to men who don't have to wear paint. The use of cosmetics embeds most women's inferiority complex, which actually enables male entitlement. "Bottom line, I am just a sex object after all," is what the Globalists want you to think. Carnal. This sets up the schisms that they can manipulate. Divide and conquer. Or as Gloria Steinem once said, "We are all bunnies." In her world, maybe so.

Indigenous women were strong and undivided and that is why they are being "transformed" as described in quote above, by the social engineers. (More in Volume 2) The goal of people like CIA Steinem is to "free" all women to become "equal" cogs in the machine. The natural gets diminished while the artificial reigns. This is what "progress" wants.

Many educated women think that they chose independently (they didn't, they were herded) to make ambition itself their priority, and then they grew too old to have kids. Other career chasers became so competitive and controlling that they could only get along with a wimp. They became wannabe patriarchs. "It's a man's world," so they became like men to gain their right to also dominate. I call this the "all male paradigm" where softness is reduced to a modality, not an ocean. And some wannabe men became dominant lesbians, with passive partners who had been molested and hurt as girls.

Human life used to have half it's population looking forward to nourishing, but now it has very few.

CIA Gloria Steinem is still lying to this day. She has been lying for 60 years.

> "Gloria Steinem says black women invented 'the feminist movement.'"
>
> *Daily Life,* March 24, 2015, 1:32PM

I guess the white suffragettes never happened. She doesn't say who co-opted the black feminists … It was the CIA, and herself, the primary agent.

Marilyn Monroe

Marilyn Monroe was one of the first "presidential models," which means mind controlled slaves. [31] She wasn't blond, nor are Madonna, Christina Aguilera, Britney Spears, or Shakira. Who is Shakira? Shakira is an Illuminati "Diva" from Colombia who claims to have 70 million Facebook followers. But in three words, she is "another corrupt phony" and not a blond. She uses the blond conditioning and furthers it. But this blond thing started with Monroe. Shakira is covered quite extensively in *Lipstick and War Crimes: Vol. 3.*

In Chapter 12 of *The Illuminati Formula to Create an Undetectable Total Mind Control Slave* by Fritz Springmeier & Cisco Wheeler, information is provided concerning Marilyn Monroe and

CIA brainwashing: "Marilyn was allowed to have no personal life, outside of the dictates of her programmers and her masters. The programmers and users bore down so hard on controlling Marilyn that they repeatedly came close to driving her insane." [32]

 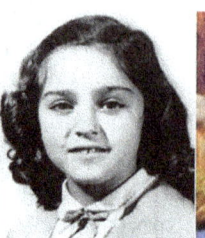   

Above, natural brunettes Marilyn Monroe and Madonna. Also not blonds, Christina Aguilera, Britney Spears, and Shakira who are being kept popular with judge stints on talent shows like American Idol (R.I.P.) and The Voice. Madonna is still doing half-time football shows for her bosses. Marilyn Monroe didn't die too soon as Ms. Magazine (see cover below) grieves, she was murdered by the CIA because she knew too much, particularly about the Kennedys. JFK didn't seduce her, she was made for him.

These later puppets are actually following the mind control protocols established with slave Monroe. "Mind control" can be covert regimes with handlers to create agents, or can refer to propaganda that brain washes and conditions society in mass. We can be tricked into worshipping blondes is perfect example. The whole blond thing is a psy-op to trigger response from masses. "Blonds have more fun" means sex. When you see a platinum blond how do you respond? Guys, is there, or is there not a sexual connotation? Ladies, is there more glamour?

Human beings can be terrorized/seduced into multiple personalities that can be used by the controllers. The scientific experimentation for this old Freemasonry system happened in Nazi Germany with Rockefeller funding.[33] While in the program, the slave is rewarded. It is a captive environment. Another presidential model, a survivor, is Cathy O'Brien who says she never was allowed to know what day it was or what time it was. She was a slave. She was conditioned to perform sexually from infancy. Her book *Trance-Formation of America* is a must read. Another Kissinger survivor's book is *Thanks for the Memories* by Bryce Taylor.

* * *

Here is as an important key point in understanding the difference between coping and *personal sovereignty* (see Glossary).

> *Stockholm Syndrome,* or capture-bonding, is a psychological phenomenon in which hostages express empathy and sympathy and have positive feelings toward their captors, sometimes to the point of defending and identifying with the captors. These feelings are generally considered irrational in light of the danger or risk endured by the victims, who essentially mistake a lack of abuse from their captors for an act of kindness.

Mind Control Out Of **Control** MK
YouTube

Cathy O'Brien speaks on mind
YouTube

Cathy O'Brien Story - Illuminati
YouTube

Cathy O'Brien: Ex-Illuminati Mind
YouTube

See more videos of **cathy o'brien mind control youtube**

Cathy O'Brien speaks on mind control PT 1 of 2 - YouTube
www.youtube.com/watch?v=-rUnC7uV5yY ▾
By goldenheartmedia's channel · 10 min · 116,199 views · Added Dec 24, 2009
Cathy O'Brien speaks of her CIA **mind control** existence and how these programs were and are being perpetrated under the illegal 1947 National Security Act ...

Cathy O'Brien: Ex-Illuminati Mind Control Victim - YouTube
www.youtube.com/watch?v=FvEBmEo4IA0 ▾
By PronStarKilluminati · 117 min · 476,073 views · Added Mar 03, 2013
Warning: Adults only, if you're easily offended don't watch Read the book here: http://static.everdot.org/ebooks/engl... For Reasons of National Security ...

Cathy O'Brien - Mind Control and Sandy Hook - YouTube
www.youtube.com/watch?v=VASWNwOKqrQ ▾
By Freeman Fly · 55 min · 98,946 views · Added Jan 15, 2013
Loughner, Holmes, Lanza, are the Powers That Be using **Mind Control** to transform America? Freeman and Frater X interview the authors of Access Denied, **Cathy** ...

Videos of thanks for the memories brice taylor

bing.com/videos

Brice Taylor - Thanks For The
YouTube

'Pedophilia No. 1 Problem In
YouTube

Brice Taylor Exposes Mind
YouTube

Brice Taylor claims Sylvestor
godlikeproductio...

The Stockholm Syndrome helps people cope. It is a prisoner's psychology. Coping involves disabling boundaries to allow the negative, while *personal sovereignty* involves maintaining boundaries to prevent the negative. The bonding that can occur in any "good old boy" environment that demands conformity, for example, is a challenge to *personal sovereignty* and integrity. One lays down one's better sense to cope with conforming to the club.

The instinct to survive as a social creature who is loyal, can be in conflict with personal survival. This is what we are facing now. If we stick with society we are doomed, because of the suicide future our leaders are leading us toward. We need to consider personal survival. Being loyal to the State that is "kind" to us is a big mistake. We each need personal boundaries, starting with the food we put into our bodies. We want pure food, for example.

With all this introduction, please study mind control. Ask yourself, "How much have I been socially engineered in secret ways, as the blond triggering exemplifies."

It is one thing to have an abusive husband. It is far worse to be a mind controlled slave like Marilyn Monroe, who can never in your life tell the truth about what you can remember, for fear you will get killed. As she was. It is also tragic to be employed and never be able to speak your mind for fear of losing your job. So we are all to some extent mind controlled, but the revelations about MK-Ultra programming may be new to the reader. Some categories of mind control which are layered in trained agents … (This training bypasses the conscious mind.)

"ALPHA: Regarded as "general" or regular programming within the base control personality; characterized by extremely pronounced memory retention, along with substantially increased physical strength [example, the Shoe Bomber] and visual acuity. Alpha programming is accomplished through deliberately subdividing the victims personality.

"BETA: Referred to as "sexual" programming. This programming **eliminates all learned moral convictions** and stimulates the primitive sexual instinct, devoid of inhibitions. "Cat" alters may come out at this level. (In Vol. 3 … Leopard skin clothing is used in Kitten Programming) (Beta is also part of Monarch programming. It involves sexualizing and addictive sex at a very young age for the victim/agent. Most actresses are beta slaves, such as Shirley MacLaine, Madonna, Beyoncé and many more. For most agents, they were molested scientifically as children, whether they become "models" or not. Oprah Winfrey was raped from age 9. She is an agent.)

"DELTA: This is known as "killer" programming, originally developed for training special agents or elite soldiers (i.e. Delta Force, First Earth Battalion, Mossad, etc.) in covert operations. Optimal adrenal output and controlled aggression is evident. Subjects are devoid of fear; very systematic in carrying out their assignment. Self-destruct or suicide instructions are layered in at this level. (Example are the two men who robbed bank in broad daylight in 1997 North Hollywood Shootout, who had been under FBI surveillance, yet allowed to proceed, who walked around robotically under fire, one killing himself because he was shot in foot, the other was allowed to bleed to death. They were programmed to do this as excuse to militarize the police. This is called a false flag operation, covered in *Lipstick and War Crimes: Vol. 5*.)

"THETA: Considered as "psychic" programming. Bloodliners (those coming from multi-generational Satanic families) determined to exhibit a greater propensity for having telepathic abilities. (or – agents discovered by almost drowning them and watching their reactions. See Davidshurter.com) Due to its evident limitations, however, various forms of electronic mind control systems were developed. (below) It is reported these are used in conjunction with highly-advanced computers and sophisticated satellite tracking systems.

"OMEGA: A "self-destruct" form of programming, also known as "Code Green." The corresponding behaviors include suicidal tendencies and/or self-mutilation. This program is generally activated when the victim/survivor begins therapy or interrogation and too much memory is being recovered. This has been reported by many MK-Ultra survivors.

"GAMMA: Another form of system protection is through "deception" programming, which elicits misinformation and misdirection. This level is intertwined with demonology and tends to regenerate itself at a later time if inappropriately deactivated."

The reader should also be aware that electronic devices of many kinds are used to mind control people. Many frequencies can be used to manage a persons brain, personality, moods, even hormones. These can be aimed from space. Obama's limousine has this kind of electronics to keep him controlled. The ELF (Extremely Low Frequency) towers (Do a search for ELF towers) across U.S. are not cell phone towers and may be about mass brain manipulation. If that sounds far fetched, look into it. The military has been studying this for 70 years.

Here is a patent talking about how to "manipulate the nervous system of the subject by pulsing images on nearby computer monitor or TV set."

| United States Patent | 6,506,148 |
| Loos | January 14, 2003 |

Nervous system manipulation by electromagnetic fields from monitors

Abstract

Physiological effects have been observed in a human subject in response to stimulation of the skin with weak electromagnetic fields that are pulsed with certain frequencies near 1/2 Hz or 2.4 Hz, such as to excite a sensory resonance. Many computer monitors and TV tubes, when displaying pulsed images, emit pulsed electromagnetic fields of sufficient amplitudes to cause such excitation. It is therefore possible to manipulate the nervous system of a subject by pulsing images displayed on a nearby computer monitor or TV set. For the latter, the image pulsing may be imbedded in the program material, or it may be overlaid by modulating a video stream, either as an RF signal or as a video signal. The image displayed on a computer monitor may be pulsed effectively by a simple computer program. For certain monitors, pulsed electromagnetic fields capable of exciting sensory resonances in nearby subjects may be generated even as the displayed images are pulsed with subliminal intensity.

Inventors: Loos; Hendricus G. (Laguna Beach, CA)
Family ID: 25359755
Appl. No.: 09/872,528
Filed: June 1, 2001

Illuminati Black Magick Tricks REVEALED!! Part 2

 The Black Child

CIA Gloria Steinem and her CIA handlers wrote a book about Marilyn Monroe. Her false story of Monroe covers up the fact that Monroe was a CIA slave. We already knew CIA Steinem was a liar, but this book about Monroe is worse. Here she is covering up true abuse, which extends to all women. CIA Steinem hates all women by not telling the true story of Marilyn Monroe.

The New World Order celebrity, Elton John, also helped hide Monroe's tragic life, with his song "Candle in the Wind." (But his handlers wrote the lyrics.) He then helped cover up the assassination of Princess Diana by singing it again at Diana's funeral. (Vol. 2, Chapter 10)

Rabbit Hole: A Satanic Ritual Abuse Survivor's Story ...

www.amazon.com › ... › Religion & Spirituality › Occult › Occultism ▼
★★★☆☆ Rating: 3.3/5 · 87 reviews · David Shurter · By **David Shurter**
Rabbit Hole: A **Satanic Ritual Abuse** Survivor's Story - Kindle edition by **David Shurter**. Download it once and read it on your Kindle device, PC, ...

David Shurter - YouTube

www.youtube.com/user/DavidShurter1 ▼
David Shurter speaks for the testify project concerning child abductions and mkultra offenses - Duration: 2 minutes, 25 seconds.

Billy Ray Cyrus in GQ: My family is under attack by Satan ...

vigilantcitizen.com › News ▼
In this startling interview with GQ, **Billy Ray Cyrus** mentions **Miley Cyrus**' "handlers", his fears of seeing her dead like Anna Nicole Smith and Michael Jackson ...

If the reader would like to jump ahead of *Lipstick and War Crimes: Vol. 3*, where I cover the real Marilyn Monroe more thoroughly, see these two webpages ...

" ... On a day in October, 1957, a woman named Lena Peritoneum was hired to take care of Marilyn Monroe. In 1979, she published her memories of the time she was the primary person taking care of Marilyn Monroe."

http://www.conspirazzi.com/marilyn-monroe-life-of-a-monarch-slave/

http://vigilantcitizen.com/vigilantreport/the-hidden-life-of-marilyn-monroe-the-original-hollywood-mind-control-slave-part-i/

KATHERINE HEPBURN

Actress and feminist legend Katherine Hepburn was touted as an independent woman, and given award after award to make her some kind of icon. However we only ever heard of her because she was funded by military-industrial-complex Howard Hughes who bought the rights of the Broadway play *Philadelphia* for her, which set her up with the funds for her "career." That is not independence. She was dependent. And why did Hughes help her of all people? Some say they had a relationship. But how did he even meet her? Well, she had parents who themselves were placed by the Rockefellers. Her family was in the club.

Hepburn's mom was Katherine Martha Houghton, a co-founder of Planned Parenthood along with Margaret Sanger. Another later Planned Parenthood head was the father of Microsoft Bill Gates, William H. Gates Sr. This is not mentioned in Wikipedia, but Bill talked about it.

Bill Gates: My Father Headed Planned Parenthood
by InfoPlanetWars
2 years ago • 5,943 views
In an appearance on NOW With Bill Moyers on May 9, 2003, th philanthropist and head of the Bill and Melinda ...
HD

(Interestingly, Globalist William Gates Sr., once head of eugenist Planned Parenthood has been a board director at Costco since 2003. That is, this Rockefeller connected billionaire controls Costco. For all it's good points, Costco cannot be trusted, and this is evident by the kind of DVD's and books they push.) Both Katherine Hepburn and Bill Gates were placed. The only reason we ever heard of either of them is that they were Rockefeller puppets dangled before us.

Planned Parenthood was not the creation of these so-called founders. All these people are *cut-outs* (See Glossary) obeying scripts written behind the scene. Sanger was a eugenist, who believed that Blacks were a racially inferior race. "Population control" for these people is about culling populations that they deem inferior. Their *disconnecting vanity* feels superior.

Racist Rockefeller minion, Planned Parenthood Margaret Sanger has been widely praised by Hillary Clinton who I introduce below.

Now the reader has a choice. Coincidence theory or conspiracy history? How do we explain that Katherine Hepburn, the daughter of Planned Parenthood founder becomes a famous actress and that the son of another Planned Parenthood "Head", Bill Gates, just happens to get the rights to market a computer operating system from IBM? Gates is continuing his father's Planned Parenthood eugenist goals with the very rich Gates Foundation that wants to "reduce world population by 15% using vaccinations and health care." (Vol. 2, Chapter 6) In fact the Co-Director of the Bill and Melinda Gates Foundation, is now Bill's father, William Sr. Isn't it just a coincidence that a former head of eugenist Planned Parenthood is now still directing eugenic programs for the Bill and Melinda Gates Foundation and helping to secretly sterilize young women of other races? (Vol. 2, Chapter 6) And, how delightful that such a monster (sorry, but what do you call someone who sterilizes girls without their knowledge) is controlling the second largest retailer in U.S., Costco. Perhaps someone who helps paralyze 47,000 children with vaccines in India (Vol. 2, Chapter 6) shouldn't be called a monster. What do you think?

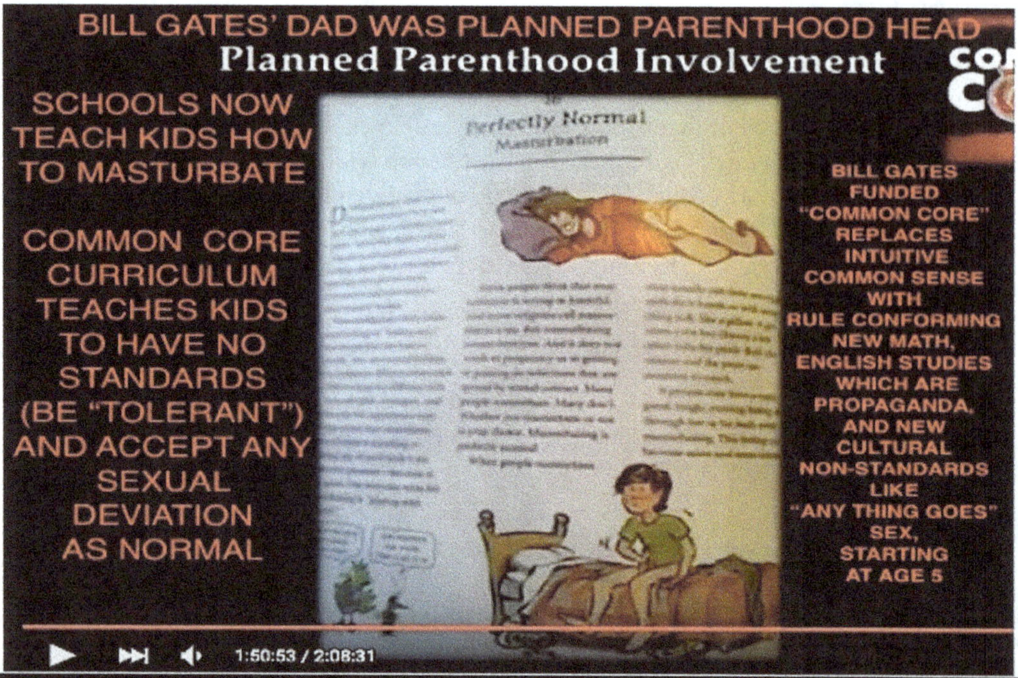
BILL GATES' DAD WAS PLANNED PARENTHOOD HEAD
Planned Parenthood Involvement
SCHOOLS NOW TEACH KIDS HOW TO MASTURBATE
COMMON CORE CURRICULUM TEACHES KIDS TO HAVE NO STANDARDS (BE "TOLERANT") AND ACCEPT ANY SEXUAL DEVIATION AS NORMAL
Perfectly Normal
BILL GATES FUNDED "COMMON CORE" REPLACES INTUITIVE COMMON SENSE WITH RULE CONFORMING NEW MATH, ENGLISH STUDIES WHICH ARE PROPAGANDA, AND NEW CULTURAL NON-STANDARDS LIKE "ANY THING GOES" SEX, STARTING AT AGE 5
1:50:53 / 2:08:31

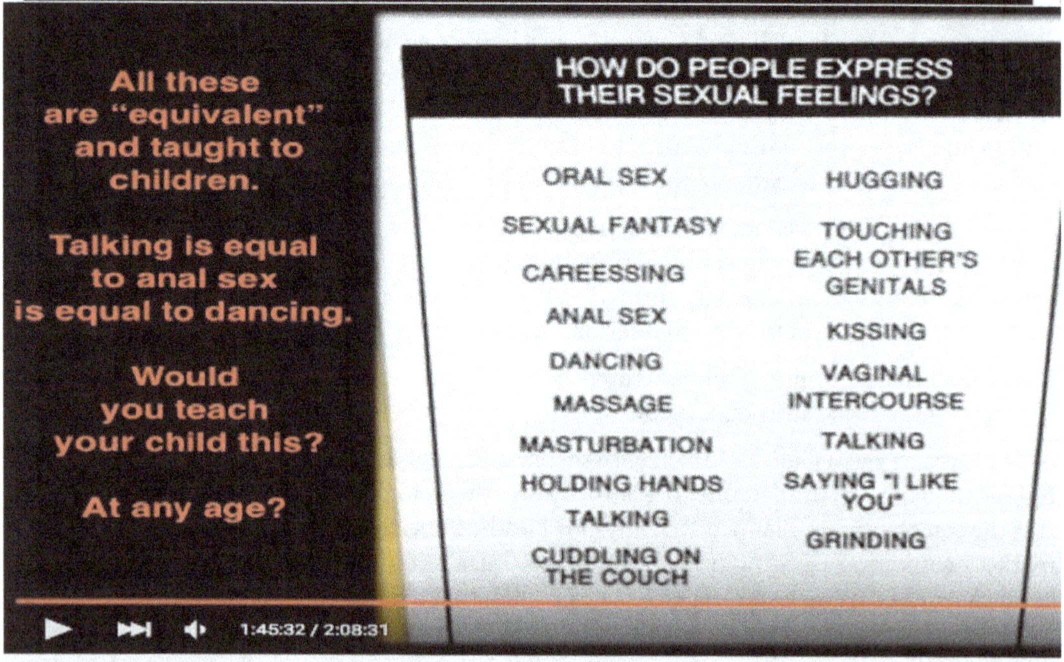
All these are "equivalent" and taught to children.
Talking is equal to anal sex is equal to dancing.
Would you teach your child this?
At any age?
HOW DO PEOPLE EXPRESS THEIR SEXUAL FEELINGS?
ORAL SEX
SEXUAL FANTASY
CAREESSING
ANAL SEX
DANCING
MASSAGE
MASTURBATION
HOLDING HANDS
TALKING
CUDDLING ON THE COUCH
HUGGING
TOUCHING EACH OTHER'S GENITALS
KISSING
VAGINAL INTERCOURSE
TALKING
SAYING "I LIKE YOU"
GRINDING
1:45:32 / 2:08:31

Brilliant anti-Common Core Speech by Dr. Duke Pesta

VisionLiberty
Subscribe 3,910

WATCH ON YOUTUBE

The "Margaret Sanger Award" (Sanger was co-founder with Hepburn's mom) in its first year was given to Carl G. Hartman, William H. Draper, Lyndon Baines Johnson, and Martin Luther King. Later recipients have included John D. Rockefeller III, Katherine Hepburn, Jane Fonda, Ted Turner and Hillary Clinton who praised Sanger. Maybe that is why Hillary got award?

The only innocent in this first year list is Martin Luther King, obviously targeted for co-option. If he had had access to her racist material, he would have never accepted award. Carl Hartman was an embryologist, invasive tech. William Draper founded Population Crisis Committee which funded Planned Parenthood, which means they gave an award to one of their own sponsors! (Draper's daughter also "coincidentally" become a known actress.) Lyndon Johnson had his deputy John Gardner destroy black communities by substituting fathers with welfare. Was that why LBJ got an award? (LBJ's John Gardener would also organize Earth Day, the idea stolen from Ira Einhorn, who was framed for murder and is still in jail to hide what he knows. [34])

How amazing that the Planned Parenthood Sanger Award was later given to Katherine Hepburn, the daughter of the co-founder of Planned Parenthood! And how about giving the award to Rockefeller when it was his own family that began the eugenics research in Nazi Germany (besides the mind control research) in the first place, and who created Planned Parenthood! And while awarding one spouse, why not award both Jane Fonda and Ted Turner? The award means nothing at all. It is just cronies having parties for each other, and crystallizing their own vanity which denies the fact that they are just cogs giving awards to their own bosses and children.

As just mentioned, Sanger Award winner Jane Fonda, yet another actress, has now set up a women's talk radio network with "Mother of Feminism" CIA Gloria Steinem. What is the association between feminism, mind control, eugenics and the CIA? Well, the Rockefellers helped fund them all. That is, they are all part of the same pyramid of abuse.

The reason Katherine Hepburn got so many Academy Awards is that award ceremonies are a technique by Globalists to affirm vanity and place standards for the public, who follow along with whomever "wins." But awards are not given for talent or service, they are given for obedience. Awards are a certification of servitude. If awards were about talent, the sponsors would lose control because any upstart could win and swing the masses in some unpredictable way. All award ceremonies are to keep the egos of the puppets feeling they are on top of the mountain.

Let's leave Hepburn for a moment to examine an up and coming "Hepburn" who is used to socially engineer the masses today. *Time Magazine* awarded 22 year old puppet Miley Cyrus as being one of the "100 Most Influential People in the World for 2014". Twenty two years old, and uneducated. Had you ever heard of "twerking" before? But it wasn't a young puppet who made this famous, it was the handlers who choreographed her whole life that brought us the one second of slutism "twerking," and then the controlled media put her on a zillion magazine covers.

When I watched her performance, it was obvious she had been specially trained to vibrate the way she did. There isn't one in a thousand women who could do what she was trained to do. She did not come up with this herself, nor the costume. Look closely at the one eye character on her outfit. Remember the one eye! She did not create this. I will be exposing celebrities in this series, not as the problem, but as the evidence of top/down control. Celebrities are talented, but their talent is used to spread a message that is not their own creation.

Time's role was to honor and spread the travesty of Miley Cyrus' behavior as the new acceptable normal. And who wrote the Cyrus story in *Time Magazine*? None other than the very objective writer Dolly Parton, her godmother, who was just fine with her godchild being a slut on stage! You can't make this stuff up.

These next words are attributed to Dolly Parton, who I very much doubt wrote them. Every single word is false. Miley Cyrus does nothing that is not scripted by her "handlers."

"If I didn't know how smart [Alpha programming] and talented Miley is, I might worry about her. But I've watched her grow up. So I don't. She knows what she's doing. [That is why she is in and out of re-hab like the other Disney brats] She was very proud of the work she did as Hannah Montana, [the ass shaking school girl] but people were gonna leave her there forever. [Impossible! Her character was a teenager!] And she was just smotherin' and chokin' in it. So she felt she had to do something completely drastic. [She did only what she was told, and choreographed nothing!] And she did. She *made her point*, she made her mark, and more power to her."

[What was the point? "I'm not a teenager anymore, I'm a porn star?" That is what her handlers wanted all her fans to see. This is called "good gone bad," a repeated script. Her job was to trash the morality of an entire generation of fans who knew her as Hannah Montana. To De-moral-ize them. Please re-read the Beta Programming description above.]

Parton continues, "Wrecking Ball" is a great song. [It is just the Stones song "Under my Thumb" with different words] The whole album is great. [Therefore, she should get most influential in world award???] So I'm hoping that now she can relax and show people how talented she really is. [She didn't relax, she has continued being a slut role model on stage. She will do any photo shoot she is told to do over and over and over again.] 'Cause the girl can write. [Dolly thinks she wrote the song!!! LOL.] The girl can sing. The girl is smart." [!]

"And she doesn't have to be so drastic. [But Dolly supports her anyway?] But I will respect her choices. I did it my way, so why can't she do it her way?"

First, none of her stuff is her choices. Second, she can do it "her way" because there are no standards, no right or wrong, anything goes, is that what you are saying Godmother? Any way is okay? Believe it or not, above was Parton's reasons why Cyrus should be named by *Time Magazine* as one of the 100 most influential people in the world 2014.

Wrecking balls Madonna and Miley Cyrus.

VOLUME 1, IGNORING THE FUTURE AND LOOKING FABULOUS   65

Above, Miley Cyrus, two years after "making her mark", still wearing anything she is told to wear, including all-seeing-eye of pyramid of abuse at 2015 VMA Awards.

MTV is really trying to make this moment "iconic". We see it appear at several occasions during the show.

Above comment by vigilantcitizen.com Sept 2, 2015. Is this the example of new normal for audience? That is what they are pushing.

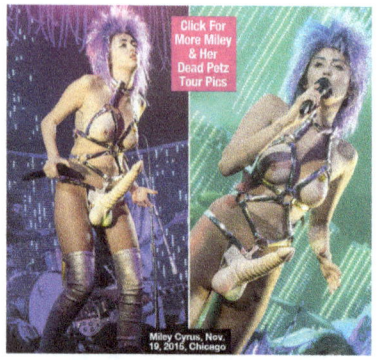

To left is Disney's Miley Cyrus, Nov. 19, 2015, bare breasted with obscene strap-on on stage. Over 2 years after Dolly Parton said that Cyrus "made her mark," she is still obeying her masters to destroy modesty and now spread trans-gender experimentation. Will *Time Magazine* award this also?

Awards are fixed. They mean nothing at all. Cyrus is now famous, not because she has talent or creative genius and deserves fame, but because the Disney machine that created her behavior, works directly with magazines like *Ms.* and *Time* to keep her center stage. They have the power to do so and they make famous whoever they want to make famous. They place these people in our minds. They create what we call "household names." That is their job, the sculpting of opinion, attitude, and docile mimicry, and the unthinking buy into it. Dear reader, you must break free or we are all lost. If *Time Magazine* has no ethical line, you must.

* * *

The exact same culture of "awards" was true for Academy Award winner, Katherine Hepburn.

Hepburn said in one of her interviews "I was raised like a man." She was raised in a highly competitive environment that replaced any nourishing side in her development, permanently making her feminine deficient.

She never had children but succeeded in the rat race, making her an archetype feminist "champion" of "independence" as created and promoted by the "we" mentioned by Rockefeller in 1906. In fact she was sponsored, not independent. I suspect she was raped as a girl, and like many women who are molested, she turned to same sex flings. Author Scotty Bowers claims that he set Katharine Hepburn up "with over 150 different women" in his book *Full Service: My Adventures in Hollywood and the Secret Sex Lives of Stars (2012)*. Gore Vidal backs Bowers' credibility. Surely Hepburn also had other pimps providing "dates." In other words, "feminist" Katherine Hepburn was a wannabe man, not a liberated woman. As a wannabe man, she even wanted women.

Again and again, we see that feminism phases with lesbianism. It is because both are anti-nature and devoted to rebellious non-convention. I am showing that this was all orchestrated by the criminal elite. The CIA is one of their spear points to coerce and pay off puppets. I cover the exact same blueprint of creation and infiltration of gay movement in Vol. 2, Chapter 10.

Globalist controlled, official-story Wikipedia says "Hepburn … refused to conform to societal [and nature's] expectations of women. She was outspoken, assertive, athletic, and wore trousers before it was fashionable [because of her example] for women to do so … With her unconventional lifestyle and the *independent characters she brought to the screen,* Hepburn came to epitomize the "modern woman" in 20th century America and helped change [normal and healthy] perceptions of women." So, there you have it, the modern woman should be unconventional. This is what CIA Steinem calls being "rebellious." Whether Hepburn was sane doesn't really matter. As long as she was unconventional.

A correction to Wikipedia—Hepburn didn't bring any characters to the screen! She was an actress! She just played the parts given to her! She appeared the way she was told to appear! And she did this for vain fame and glory, as we will see. Virtue and modesty go together but Hepburn and Cyrus and Steinem don't know about this. You see, virtue is our innocence, so virtue is naturally modest. To destroy our innocence with brash outspoken "attitude" cuts our ability to be good. We are too busy being vain.

In the song "Sugar," popular band Maroon 5 calls modesty "shy shit." That is because the song is all about lust, not love. We trash modesty. Girls are supposed to have attitude like hardened street whores. Modesty and virtue gone. This is the elite's agenda. Empowering women should be about protecting modesty so women can remain true women, and not become "empowered" to act like tough men.

Katherine Hepburn was an early wrecking ball. As a puppet, her job was to establish the new "modern" in her time. In that process, innocence and the true feminine was attacked, and has been attacked since, with the newest puppet being Miley Cyrus.

Breaking eggs, breaking ovaries, breaking roles, and men are supposed to suddenly become passive and shut down in some chivalrous way so that women can act domineering.

In the world of cooperation there is a recognition of specialized qualities, and as most women are womanly, and most men are manly, we have natural polarity. In my opinion the polarity became institutionalized and abusive. The early feminists were correct to point this out. Men were not secure in their masculinity because they themselves were slaves coming out of a European feudal pecking order, so they took it out on their women. That is, they weren't natural men. They were dysfunctional with a chip on their shoulder. They were abused and taking it out on someone weaker. Polarity became abusive. The problem with force is that limits are needed, or force becomes destructive. That is where religion has always stepped in. If you think about it, religion is about controlling men, because women are naturally more gentle.

The reason that the Japanese soldiers were so monstrously brutal in World War II is that they were all abused slaves. Who colonized the world? Indentured servants. So the abuse by men of women is not found in "human nature," it is found in dysfunctional slave societies ruled by an oppressive elite. What kind of people would bind the feet of their wives! Not Chinese peasants but Chinese elite! We don't see gross distortion of gender roles in indigenous cultures that are natural and close to nature, we see differentiation, specialization and cooperation.

A correction to male abusiveness by unnatural Western men was needed. Brave humanitarian whistleblower women came forward. New Zealand has nothing to be proud of about this, as New Zealand and Australia are *social engineering* petri dishes. If the New World Order didn't back (and co-opt) woman's suffrage it never would have happened. It was allowed first in New Zealand as a testing ground for the reasons stated in video above about Rockefeller Feminism.

New Zealand laws were controlled then and now. New Zealand and Australia are not sovereign countries, but for that matter, neither is UK or U.S. Another wave of humanitarian whistleblowers was the Black feminists mentioned above who were ambushed by CIA Gloria Steinem.

Co-opted second-wave feminism wanted to *spread the desire to dominate* into the minds of women, as we see in Hepburn image above. (Please see books *Who Stole Feminism?* and *The War Against Boys* by Christina Hoff Sommers.)

In the same interview as the "raised like a man" quote, Hepburn said that in her opinion a career was incompatible with raising children. This was honest! She said flat out a woman could not be both a professional and a good mother. "You can do one or the other. You can't do both." Well, she nailed it on that, which for some reason was not remembered as a warning to other "feminists." I think this is called selective amnesia.

In a rare and truthful article in *Forbes Magazine*, "Don't Marry Career Women" by Michael Noer, the reasons to avoid career women were listed and scholastic studies were cited. When this *Forbes* critique came out, the false pride of career women went ballistic. The heat was so strong that *Forbes* then only posted the Noer article along side of the rebuttal. The politically correct security guards wouldn't let the article stand alone! The rebuttal however, only underscores and confirms what Noer pointed out. Amazing. The rebuttal article starts by ignoring all the studies Noer cites. "Don't confuse me with facts" is the attitude it starts with. It ends with "So, guys, if you're *game* for an *exciting* life, go ahead and marry a professional gal."

This is exactly the reason men should avoid marrying a "professional gal" because the foundation of good relationships is not consuming "exciting" games, but cultivating service and character together.

The implication in quote above is that marrying a non-career woman will be boring, as Hillary's cookie quote (coming up) also states. The writer was superior after all. In the world of disconnected entitlement, life is not profound or connected or sacred, life is a game, and we are supposed to seek *excitement* as fast as possible, and have disdain for those other boring people who aren't on the fast train.

Life is really not a game though. Those who think so are killing the planet. The game of the masses who are guided by these social engineers, is to consume as much as possible to prove status and "success." From the top "chessmen" Globalists, to the "professional," to the average consumer, life is treated by many as an artificial game with no real consequences to future generations.

"if you obey all the rules, you miss all the fun."

– katharine hepburn

I haven't found a quote of Hepburn that emphasizes sacrifice or purification. As an entitled "anything goes," let's break rules for the fun of it, same-sex prostitute user, I wouldn't expect it from her. As a "feminist" she seems to be remembered as utterly self-absorbed and indulgent, but this is framed as model behavior. As an Ethiopian friend told me, "modesty doesn't fit into corporate culture because you are supposed to push yourself forward." For advice in the image to left, controlled Hollywood put Hepburn on a pedestal. "Breaking is fun, sustaining is boring." This is the front door to illicit immoral corruption. If she had obeyed the rules, she might have missed her fun sexual addiction with 150 strangers. Hepburn wasn't woman enough to be with a man. She was not whole. She was damaged, probably as I said, from childhood molestation.

The New World Order, a term fully outed in Vol. 2, Chapter 1, hates self-sufficient traditional communities that are independent from their control. Tradition is in the way of their hegemony. The building blocks of ancient community are *families who obey rules*. So this explains the CIA "rebellion" against traditional standards. We were taught that rebelling for it's own sake is "fun" and there are no consequences. Again, this is the "anything goes" non-ethic.

Banner to right looks like a joke spoof, but it describes what has occurred. In my opinion, a real woman has a quiet essence within. Most "modern" women have bought the noisy conditioning to become donkeys chasing the carrot of "excitement," as encouraged by placed people like Katherine Hepburn and CIA Gloria Steinem and the woman who wrote rebuttal for the *Forbes* article, and the thousands of ads with mouths wide open. In other words, being "liberated" is tied to titillation, consumerism, and "freedom" from rules, such as right and wrong! Ultimately, such freedom becomes licentious experimentation with lust as king, I mean, queen. :)

Free West Papua
Suluama Fuimaono-Sapolu

The statement, "So, guys, if you're *game* for an *exciting* life, go ahead and marry a professional gal," quite clearly displays conceit and false pride. *Indigenous women* aren't proud of being women, they don't have to be. They are just themselves. They don't have to prove anything. Indulgent vanity, "independence", and arrogant false pride is like an infection that starts killing off a woman's feminine side. Then, as an amputee, she can only offer a man a part-time relationship.

Within the mind of an "independent women" is not "I am woman", but rather, "I must prove I am also a real man by being loyal first and above all else, to my career." In other words, this kind of career-woman has a chip on her shoulder. She must prove something. She must prove to her *social engineering* handlers that she is fulfilling the program of trying not to be feminine. Her bottom line is to be a good slave for industrial society and have a successful career in that slave system. The men and women of Papua New Guinea are not considered real people, you see, because they don't have a career. Dear reader, their lifestyle is much more real than the unsustainable civilization you are taking part in. A sustainable lifestyle is superior, not "primitive."

For young men reading this, if you are attracted to someone and she tells you she is studying to be a doctor or a lawyer or any high investment career ambition, just close your eyes, slowly turn your head, let your shoulders start to turn, turn on your heel, and … start walking. She is already married. She is not wearing a wedding band, but she is already married. You and your future family will come second. She has something more important to do. She is deeply committed to this prior relationship. She is an "equal" in the rat race, after all. Professional women and some college girls reading this might wince. It is true.

In nature men hunt to feed everyone. It isn't fun. It isn't titillating. It is work. Very hard work and dangerous. Anyone who is addicted to their career for "fun" has forgotten that we work so that we can have something to eat, we don't eat so we can work.

Vain industry clad slaves in merchandise status trance being successful in unsustainability. They are wearing slacks, a la wrecking ball, Katherine Hepburn

Hepburn is a splendid example of the nazi-feminist "independent" woman, liberated from feeling that feminine nourishing is a reward in itself. She was asked what to do with old people who had been abandoned in nursing homes. She responded, "Shoot em, shoot em!" What else would a femi-nazi say? Gosh Katherine. Was it beneath you to take care of people?

(Just for the record, I've diaper trained two kids and am now primary caretaker of my mom. Abandoning others is the industrial pyramid-of-abuse system, not our human system. The reason I had two failed marriages is because I was part of a concocted culture that "rebelled" against chastity and long courtship. We were "free" after all. I married twice based on lustful need. Giant mistake, but seen as "normal" by the feminist culture I grew up in. I know now, sex before marriage is a bad idea. The lust of Hollywood succeeded, giving me two broken marriages, and I have been a single dad, twice. I still am.)

One of Hepburn's first movies, *Desk Set* (1957), begins to set women up for their choice to become dominant culture contractors, rather than the nourishing feminine pole of the human species.

Hepburn avoided Academy Award ceremonies and some interpreted this as her being independent. She later admitted that the reason she didn't go was that she was afraid to lose! In other words, she was utterly vain.

Answer: Every one when women mimic males.

VOLUME 1, IGNORING THE FUTURE AND LOOKING FABULOUS

To be "independent" means to be a lone jaguar, no longer a social team creature. This is inhuman, and therefore, an "independent woman" or "independent man" is an oxymoron. (An oxymoron is an impossible combination of words that, when practiced, is utterly dysfunctional.) Being "independent" came with anonymous "freedom" of city life. This is exactly what Big Brother wants in our heads, to feel "free" about being disconnected. No one can be "independent" and also human.

Hepburn wrote an autobiography entitled *Me, Stories of My Life*. Me me me.

MADONNA (AND PEAS IN POD, SHIRLEY MACLAINE AND MILEY CYRUS)

The singer known as Madonna was and is a scripted, programmed, CIA slave. She did not rise from the dust, she was groomed. (More in Chapter 8). I only mention her briefly here. The use of the name "Madonna" co-opts the faith of Latin America. When we hear that name, we now think of the wrecking ball singer, not the mother of Jesus. I am correct, yes?

There was nothing very special about her. Her voice, her dancing, her looks, none was that special. She was simply programmed, funded and placed to be outrageous and her ego was juiced to believe she was significant. What was special was that she was the first international beta programmed slave to really be well marketed. CIA Madonna is now the richest woman in the music industry, with over a billion dollars. That was the Madonna Operation. She was used for a *social engineering* mission, which was to destroy roles, and even destroy the idea that anything can be wrong. In her world, as we shall see in Vol 2: Chapter 8, there is no right or wrong. This is the "satanist" thread, which I thought was just hysterical labeling until I studied it. Satanism is a real club with real victims. Satanism means anti-goodness with real members.

Madonna was one of the first international "wrecking balls," a role that Disney brat Miley Cyrus has now been assigned. Please see Glossary "cage theme."

International twerking instructor Miley Cyrus, loved by a generation of girls as Hannah Montana, is a mind controlled puppet/victim, seen above with CIA Obama shirt. Her handlers made her slavery normalized/integrated by having her do a photo shoot of her own victimization. She absolutely did not design the shirt on right. She is sticking out her tongue as her trade mark trashy look in photo shoot. Her handlers gave her the shirt. Obama was placed by same Cabal that is placing Cyrus. Slave Cyrus is helping place slave Obama. Same club, same masters.

Katrina - Wrecking Ball (The Voice Kids 2014: Finale)

The wrecking ball is now being pushed as acceptable. To left we see a young talent show contestant on *The Voice* for kids, singing the Cyrus song "Wrecking Ball" with same staging, to make sure everyone remembers Cyrus's nude performance. Is it appropriate to sexualize children with a new normal that borders on pornography? Behind contestant is the satanic five pointed star, which we will review several times. Think the Pentagon. This five pointed star appeared in the medal given to Steinem above. We see the Illuminati star pushed in old Popeye cartoon below with green subliminal penis, and horns, no less. I very much doubt that the Kratts brothers created all the images in their popular children's series.

We see the star, we see the inappropriate sex, we see their show pushing transhumanism (enhancing people with machines and electronics) in every cartoon, which follows informative natural history pieces to suck in the children. *Social engineering now starts in infancy, more in Volume 2.*

* * *

Dear reader, please remember this axiom; fame isn't earned, it is funded. Famous people are made famous because they are greedy malleable chess pieces. However, more reliable than buying off someone is to groom them from childhood, like Churchill, FDR, Kissinger, Gates, Clinton, Gore, Bush, Spears, Aguilera, Gomez, Lovato, Cyrus, Madonna, Winfrey, ad nauseum.

If someone is famous, *they were made famous by the machine.* One hundred years ago in 1915, JP Morgan bought editorial rights to the top 25 U.S. Newspapers. We have not had free press for a century. This controlled media promotes the controlled actors on the political and entertainment stages. Uncooperative artists are smeared with horrible photos or leaks about their personal lives and their careers are flattened. Charlie Sheen was attacked for questioning the 9/11 official story. [35] *Fame is either groomed, allowed, or disallowed.* Those attached to fame are constantly threatened with being cut off if they don't come willingly to party after party.

Madonna has had continual programming all her life. Just as Gloria Steinem had "boy friends" who were CIA handlers, so did Madonna. Warren Beatty's role has not been examined enough. The following excerpt is from *Illuminati Bloodlines* by Fritz Springmeier.

"Warren Beatty. (b. 1937 in VA)—This actor is from the Illuminati Beatty family and starred in Disney's *Dick Tracy*. The *Dick Tracy* film uses color in a special way, and this ties in with the color programming of the mind-control. Some total mind-controlled slaves have programming based on Disney's *Dick Tracy* movie for them to track down and kill "targets" (people). **Warren's sister is the famous (or infamous) Shirley MacLaine.** Shirley "MacLaine" is not what she appears. Her father was a professor who was a CIA asset. She was used by the CIA as a sex slave. She became popular with the studios because she went to bed with the correct people. Her talents [dancing, acting] were used to get her, as an intelligence slave, into places that an obvious intelligence agent couldn't go. She was married to a man in the NSA for nearly 20 years. Her adopted name MacLaine [reportedly her mother's maiden name] is a pun on McLain, VA where the CIA programmed her. She was used by the CIA in an operation in Australia, where the CIA used her as a sex slave to compromise Andrew Peacock, an Australian MP, so that they could establish the Nugen-Hand bank for their dirty money laundering etc. She is friends with satanist Stephen Nance who has provided her with some of her teachings. Lowell McGovern writes her material. The CIA has programmed many of their New Age slaves to adore Shirley MacLaine. [As another generation would be taught to adore Madonna or Cyrus, or to worship the slave Beyoncé.]

"An example of this is Christa Tilton, one of their mind-controlled slaves, who revealed in an interview how she considered herself a born-again Christian who had spent most of her life in Oklahoma, but had mysteriously been drawn to Shirley MacLaine. During her life she has gotten repeated "psychic urgings"—that is strong urges to do things and go places, which she doesn't understand where these urgings came from. After hypnosis, Christa drew pictures of the doctor who programmed her. Christa has had a federal agent monitor her constantly. Her husband has seen this agent, who has shown up on her door step and made calls to her. She names the agent John Wallis (most likely a cover name). This agent has a complete knowledge of her life, and government agents have taken photos of her during her supposedly "alien abduction" experiences. Christa is just one of hundreds of victims who have been programmed to adore Shirley MacLaine. (Christa is mentioned here because she is one case that this author is familiar with.) Warren Beatty … was a student at the Stella Adler Theater Studio in NYC … "

– Fritz Springmeier

Assuredly, Warren Beatty, brother of Shirley MacLaine with a CIA father, and 19 years older than Madonna, was more than Madonna's boyfriend. His sister was trained as a sexual agent, and he was trained as a handler. He programmed thousands of beta kittens. Unsurprisingly, Beatty's daughter is trans-gender; the unnatural demonic unfolds. If the above seems like hearsay about Shirley MacLaine, who herself probably can't remember her programming, because this is what MK-Ultra programming accomplishes, the story above is backed up by this following account from her own daughter, about MacLaine's disconnected, disassociated sense of values.

> MacLaine's daughter Sachi Parker, now 54, a mother of two in Westchester County, N.Y., wrote that her movie-star mom pressured her to lose her virginity to a 1970s boyfriend, while a pair of sex therapists [handlers] was staying at their Malibu home. [They had NO respect for her innocence.] "We're all here to help you, sweetheart," MacLaine

said, according to Parker, who claims she felt "like Mia Farrow surrounded by Satanists in *Rosemary's Baby*." [!] After having unprotected sex while [Mommy] MacLaine waited in a nearby room, the couple purportedly emerged to a waiting audience. "Did you achieve climax?" the sex therapists asked, according to Parker. "We both nodded vigorously. They smiled smugly. I hated them."

– From book *Lucky Me, 2013,* by Sachi Parker

I include this because Sachi Parker speaks for all young women world wide. She experienced the *disconnecting vanity* of people who want to manipulate natural innocence and push uncommitted sex on youngsters as a cultural normal, when this has not existed anywhere, ever. She lost her chance to share her innocence and therefore her heart and trust, with someone in a committed meaningful relationship. Her elders were more concerned with nerve endings than spirit. They wanted to know if me, me, me was satisfied. Only physical satisfaction considered. She was right to hate them, and was courageous enough to voice that anger, almost 40 years later. Think about that suffering for a moment. She felt molested and never got over it. There is a whole generation who should feel the same. I do. I wish I hadn't had sex as a teenager. I wish I had a whole family.

In her response to her daughter's book, at least publicly, Shirley MacLaine seems to be annoyed that her daughter questioned show business. MacLaine called her daughter *dishonest*. Who is dishonest however? Like Hepburn, MacLaine did not create her career, she obeyed. She did not create the scene below of the Illuminati Pyramid and all-seeing-eye in the movie she starred in. (*Being There*, 1979) She was a puppet of the Illuminati entertainment industry and the CIA. She bedded who she was told to bed. She did not create the yellow salacious poster of the second movie, which clearly portrays beta slave and handler, or choose the dancing photo below which could hardly not be seen as risque. She just went along. Is she accountable or not? Did she or did she not sell women as sex objects? Who is she? Did she abandon her daughter or not? Who is she? *Like CIA Gloria Steinem, MacLaine "dated" Henry Kissinger!* Kissinger used her and furthered her programming. And her brother "dated" Madonna.

The actors and actresses don't create the staging, but they willingly participate. By ignoring the manipulation of themselves, they ignore many other things. They ignore what they portray, how they impact culture, what they represent. They are disassociated.

Sachi Parker ... "I try to understand her," she told *20/20*. "I find myself wanting to protect her so badly, because I so love her [Stockholm Syndrome] ... And yet the pain is very deep. I would hope that she would own it and apologize. That would really, really be wonderful."

Later in her life, Shirley MacLaine wrote a book *Out On a Limb*, about her exploration of spirituality. I won't make any comment on the content here. Because MacLaine has multiple personalities, we have to step back a bit to see if she actually even wrote the book. It is much more likely that the book was part of the New Age Operation. The fact that network TV produced a show based on her book, says that the Illuminati controlled industry was behind her, which should be no surprise. She was a change agent her whole life. Three of the arms of wrecking ball *social engineering* are Feminism, New Age, and Gay. A fourth is the Galactic Federation mob.

Back to Madonna (I quote Madonna, in Vol. 2, Chapter 8.) We can be sure Madonna's children will have stories someday, and hopefully sooner than later. Madonna, as we will learn, is very unlike Sachi Parker. Madonna is proud to have had no mother. She even attributes her "success" to having no mother. (Vol. 2, Chapter 8) This would be accurate however, as parentless girls like CIA Steinem, CIA Fonda, and CIA Madonna make easy pickings for covert predators looking for new agents who they make fabulously successful.

The reason all these people are important, is the culture says they are important, and we conform to that culture. They are the role models of youth. Whether we like/follow these people or not, we are impacted and "transformed" by the culture they lead with their roles because of the fame which the machine gives them. They are not just celebrities, they are programs. I am into deprogramming, not celebrity gossip. If the reader adores any of these people wake up! Your adoration was a manipulated outcome.

Hillary Clinton

" ... I want to be that champion. You don't have to get by. You can get ahead, and stay ahead."

– Hillary Clinton, campaign words, 2015.

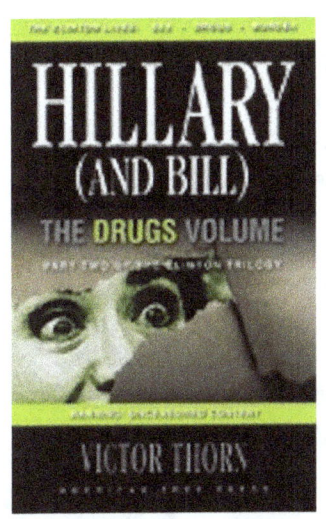

Does that sound like any understanding of sustainability? Who does one stay ahead of? Since when can any policy make someone a winner? Ahead on the welfare line? There are 47 million Americans on food stamps with NO plan for them doing anything but "getting by." Nor is there any possible plan if wealth is to be concentrated by "professionals" and labor outsourced to other countries. Hillary Clinton has no plan. She and her husband are 1% Globalists who serve the 1%. Hillary Clinton is just blowing smoke.

The three volume series by Victor Thorn reveals the vast profits made by Clintons when drugs were run through Mena airport in Arkansas for the Nicaragua Contra campaign.

I only mention Hillary because she is running for President as an alleged liberated woman, who would be in jail for life if the truth came out. Hillary Clinton is a bisexual [36] cocaine user, and sex slave abuser [37] who, like her serial rapist [38] and drug lord [39] husband Bill, is incapable of saying anything honest.

Here is a partial list of confirmed rapes or near rapes by Bill Clinton: Kathleen Willey, Glencola Sullivan, Gennifer Flowers, Janet Holman, Paula Jones, Eileen Wellstone, Juanita Broaddrick, Elizabeth Ward, Carolyn Moffet, Paula Corbin, Sandra Allen James, Christy Zercher, Kathleen Willey.

Most of the raped women expressed fear of speaking because of the Clintons' vindictive reputation. Here you will find the long list of people connected with Clintons who suspiciously died. [40] The following four men were Clinton's body guards and assigned to the 1993 Waco, Texas standoff. Steve Willis, Robert Williaoms, Conway LeBleu, Todd McKeehan.

> "According to Linda Thompson, videotapes and other evidence indicates that none died from guns fired by Branch Davidians. [All were government assassinations.] In his address to employees of the Treasury Department in the Cash Room on March 18, 1993, Clinton said: "My prayers and I'm sure yours are still with the families of all four of the Alcohol, Tobacco and Firearms agents who were killed in WACO—Todd McKeehan and Conway Le Bleu of New Orleans; Steve Willis of Houston, and Robert Williams *from my hometown of Little Rock.* Three of those four were assigned to my security during the course of the primary or general election." However, the Little Rock, Arkansas office of the ATF confirmed that all four had at one point been bodyguards for Bill Clinton, three while he was campaigning for President, and while he had been governor of Arkansas. In the videotape by the American Justice Federation, "WACO II, the Big Lie Continues," Linda Thompson demonstrates that 15 shots were fired from six separate weapons into and out of a room into which three of the four agents had entered through a window. Four of these shots were fired from an overhead helicopter, an agent outside the window, firing an MP5 submachine gun, who also threw in a concussion grenade, fired at least two shots into the room. In the autopsies of these agents, three had virtually identical wounds to the left temple that exited through the rear of the head, execution-style. A "private physician" treated all four." [41]

Does this imply that the Clintons had these men killed because they knew too much? Yes it does. I'll add two more of the long list of scores of people and then I'll stop.

> Died 1986: Judy Gibbs (along with her sister Sharon) appeared in the December 1979 issue of *Penthouse,* and later worked at a bordello near Mena, Arkansas which also ran a blackmail operation with photos taken of the customers with their girls. According to the Gibbs family, Bill Clinton was a regular customer of Judy. While cooperating with law enforcement in a drug investigation, Judy was burned alive when her house burned down. In a sworn statement, Clinton bodyguard Barry Spivey related how he had been with the governor when the governor's plane had flown over Judy Gibb's house and Clinton had shown Judy's *Penthouse* photos on the plane and pointed out the house."

> Gary Johnson: Not dead, but beaten near death and left for dead. Had videotapes of Clinton entering Gennifer Flowers' apartment. His tapes were taken. [42]

WACO 1993, BILL CLINTON BECOMES PRESIDENT.

For those unfamiliar with the Waco tragedy of 1993; families in a Waco, Texas church compound were accused of killing four police persons when scores of law enforcement personnel stormed their buildings without warning. The deaths resulted in a siege, and finally, 86 church members died in a fire that they themselves allegedly set. They "committed suicide" was the lie.

In the well documented youtube "Waco–A New Revelation" we learn that newly elected Bill Clinton sent military helicopters (below image) to Waco Texas to machine gun members of Branch Davidian sect. We see videos of machine gun used with incendiary devices to start the fires, but investigators say most of the people found dead were in fact shot. Incendiary devices were found in the burned rubble (image next page). The women and children who were hiding in a church vault were all killed with a single shape-charge bomb placed on the concrete ceiling. The steel rebar is bent downward (image above).

Waco - A New Revelation

Bill Clinton could not have organized all this so quickly by himself. He was placed as a "Democrat" to give an illusion of change. Former Mk-ultra White House sex slave, Cathy O'Brien, witnessed Bush Sr. and Bill Clinton conversing with same exact philosophy as early as 1984, 8 years before the two ran

Waco II, The Big Lie Continues

against each other for President. From the administrations of Bush Sr. to Clinton to Bush Jr. to Obama, the U.S. has had one seamless crime syndicate in power. Now Hillary Clinton is running for President and as of this writing, just stole the primary in New Hampshire from Bernie Sanders. Vietnam traitor John McCain (See youtube The Truth About John McCain, American Traitor) and Skull and Cross Bones fraternity member John Kerry ran for office against Bush Jr. and Obama, in the now typical election where both candidates are placed and are indistinguishable from each other as puppets under the international New World Order.

The Clintons had Bill's bodyguards conveniently killed because they knew too much about his sordid and criminal past. Their deaths by Delta Force were blamed on the church members which initiated the siege. Soon afterwards the White House chief counsel, Vince Foster, "committed suicide." The youtube shows the fallacies of this "suicide." Maggie Williams, Clinton's chief of staff, removed evidence about Waco from Counsel Foster's office.

Waco - A New Revelation

Linda Tripp - Hillary Ordered Waco Slaughter
2/11/2001

http://citizenwells.net/2015/07/30/linda-tripp-hillary-directed-waco-bill-abused-monica-newsmax-february-10-2001-hillary-clinton-pressured-vince-foster-to-resolve-1993-waco-standoff-monica-lewinsky-more-of-a-victim-of-bill-clinton/

Hillary Clinton pressured the late [White House Chief Counsel] Vince Foster to resolve the 1993 Waco standoff in a move that led to the deaths of more than 80 men, women and children, former White House aide Linda Tripp charged in an interview Friday night. Tripp also alleged that Monica Lewinsky was more of a victim of Bill Clinton's sexual predations than the former White House intern has publicly acknowledged. Appearing on CNN's "Larry King Live," Tripp suggested that Foster, at Mrs. Clinton's direction, transmitted the order to move on the Branch Davidian's Waco compound, which culminated in a military-style … attack on the wooden structure.

… Tripp described Foster's demeanor as "dignified, decent, caring, smart" during his early days at the White House. But when Waco happened, she said, "that's when I first knew that Vince was falling apart." Foster was found shot to death in a Virginia park three months later.

Tripp said she was with the former deputy White House counsel when the news of the Waco assault broke on television. "A special bulletin came on showing the atrocity at Waco and the children. And his face, his whole body slumped, and his face turned white, and he was absolutely crushed knowing—knowing the part he had played. And he had played the part at Mrs. Clinton's direction," charged Tripp.

Tripp was stunned by the contrast between Foster's heartfelt emotion at the Waco tragedy and what she observed from Mrs. Clinton. "Her reaction, on the other hand, was heartless," Tripp told King, adding, "I can only tell you what I saw."

When asked how the decision to move on Waco was transmitted, Tripp said, "Foster, Mrs. Clinton, [deputy Attorney General] Webb Hubbell, [Attorney General] Janet Reno."

Tripp's new charge corroborates allegations first leveled in the 1999 documentary on the deadly confrontation, "Waco: A New Revelation." In the film, director Michael McNulty included the account of former House Waco investigator T. March Bell. "One of the interesting things that happens in an investigation is that you get anonymous phone calls," Bell explains in the film. "And we in fact received anonymous phone calls from Justice Department managers and attorneys who believe that pressure was placed on Janet Reno by Webb Hubbell, pressure that came *from the first lady of the United States."* [Hillary Clinton had had the bodyguards murdered and was growing nervous as the Waco Siege lengthened. She wanted all evidence destroyed and it was destroyed.]

At the film's premiere, Bell told NewsMax.com that phone logs obtained by House investigators indicated that *Mrs. Clinton*, Foster and Hubbell worked on Waco together. "Those phone logs were Webb Hubbell's phone logs. There were calls from the first lady and Vince Foster to Webb Hubbell's office" during the Waco crisis, he said.

Bell said Mrs. Clinton grew more and more impatient as the Waco standoff came to dominate the headlines during the early months of the Clinton administration. It was she, Bell's source claims, who pressured a reluctant Janet Reno to act. Reno, on the other hand, was not enthusiastic about launching the assault, said Bell. "Give me a reason not to do this," she is said to have begged aides ... also http://rense.com/general8/tripp.htm

Linda Tripp Breaks 20-Year Silence by William Bigelow, Daily Mail, 7/29/2015

Linda Tripp, the woman who exposed Monica Lewinsky as Bill Clinton's mistress but has remained silent the last twenty years about what she knew about Bill and Hillary Clinton, gave an exclusive interview to The Daily Mail in which she offered what she knew about Hillary Clinton that makes her unfit for the presidency. During the bimbo eruptions [affairs and rapes by Bill] Hillary 'destroyed women so that their stories never saw the light of day,' Tripp says. She went from being a lackluster First Lady with unimpressive approval numbers to First Victim because of Monica Lewinski affair. Hillary will stop at nothing to achieve her end - the Presidency - and sees the public as plebians easily seduced into believing her, says Tripp.

Tripp sat outside the Oval Office the first three months of the Clinton Administration, then moved to an office directly adjacent to Hillary's second floor West Wing office until Tripp left the administration. She told the *Daily Mail* that to Hillary, her election as president would "be part of a coronation instead of an election," adding, "I think the most compelling thing about Hillary is that she will stop at nothing to achieve her end and that she views the public as plebeians easily seduced into believing her point of view."

Tripp continued, "Hillary Clinton ruled the White House even as early as 1993 and **every scandal that originated in the Clinton administration was the brainchild of Hillary.** When I think of Hillary Clinton I think of a lingering taint of scandal and wrong doing and, in my opinion, possible criminal activity."

Tripp pointed out, "As is widely acknowledged, Hillary took care of all the 'bimbo eruptions' of which there were thousands in order to present to the world an electable candidate. In this endeavor she was ruthless. She destroyed women so that their stories never saw the light of day." She noted that Hillary orchestrated the marginalizing of Gennifer Flowers, who said in 1992 that she and Bill Clinton had been lovers for 12 years [and that Hillary was a lesbian].

Tripp, of course, was quite familiar with the Monica Lewinsky affair, and stated, "Hillary was not only aware of Monica Lewinsky, she ensured that Monica was removed from the White House and in the end Hillary went from being a lackluster First Lady with unimpressive approval numbers to wronged wife. Literally within the blink of an eye she propelled herself to First Victim status. This turned the corner for Hillary."

Tripp pointed out that Hillary's later career was predicated on her reaction to the Lewinsky affair. She said, "Women across the world could certainly understand her position of standing by her man, finding it admirable that she was working on her marriage, unaware that it was a charade. **She has that particular scandal to thank for her Senate candidacy and election and for everything that followed."**

Still, Tripp insisted that the "bimbo issues" of Bill Clinton obscured the most important issue. She asserted, "In the case of Monica Lewinsky the story was never really about Monica or Linda Tripp. It was about subornation of perjury and obstruction of justice and a true abuse of power on the part of a sitting president. That should have been the story. It never was. And so it gave Monica her much needed fifteen minutes and it took the rest of us along with it but the actual crux of the entire issue escaped most. And now the very person who orchestrated that cover up and all the other cover ups over the years including those surfacing today is running for president of the United States."

Tripp took time to discuss the Whitewater scandal, which broke in 1994 and revolved around real-estate purchases involving the Clintons in 1978 when Bill was attorney general of Arkansas. Tripp said what she saw the Clintons do in 1994 "was not spin. It was lying to the American people knowingly and doing it routinely."

In 2001 [the title of this article, "20 year silence" should have been 14 year silence], Tripp told CNN Host Larry King that Hillary Clinton pressured the late **Vince Foster,** former deputy White House counsel, to resolve the Waco standoff problem in 1993. Former House Waco investigator T. March Bell charged that Hillary pressured Attorney General Janet Reno through Deputy Attorney General Webb Hubbell to initiate the attack on the Waco compound in 1993 that left 86 people dead, including children. Bell charged that Hillary orchestrated the action because the Waco standoff was dominating the news.

Tripp concluded about Hillary Clinton, "I watched her on countless occasions blatantly lie to the American people and knowingly lie."

… The year 1994 saw the first of a series of investigations into the propriety of real-estate purchases involving Bill and Hillary back in 1978 when he was attorney general of Arkansas and shortly before he became governor.

The investigations spanned seven years and became known as the Whitewater Scandal after the name of the business Bill and Hillary had started with friends James B. and Susan McDougal with the intention of developing 230 acres of land in the Ozarks, Arkansas. According to Tripp what she witnessed behind the scenes at the peak of the Whitewater scandal 'was not spin. It was lying to the American people knowingly and doing it routinely.' She said that not for the first time and certainly not for the last: 'This was not recognizing any controlling legal authority investigating the various scandals and obstructing the investigations at every turn to ensure the malfeasance never surfaced publicly.'

'This was not a mistake or error or even spin. This was pure manipulation of the truth. In a press conference during the height of the Whitewater frenzy **she was well rehearsed, her wardrobe was carefully selected to be soft and pastel and essentially every word out of her mouth, preserved for posterity, was a lie.** It's all of a piece with Hillary.'

Because according to Tripp, Hillary operates on the assumption that, 'the rules do not apply' to her or her husband. Her modus operandi was, and continues to be, Tripp explained: 'I will do what I want and then when I'm questioned I will say, "oops," or "bureaucratic snafu", and then after a couple of months her refrain will be, "this is old news, it's been investigated, I did nothing wrong, let's move on, it's time to address the issues facing the middle class of America."

'That's what she has always done and that's what she will continue to do and the frightening aspect of that approach is that it works.'

It is, Tripp believes, the way Hillary is approaching emailgate, the current scandal in which she is embroiled and which centers on the fact that, throughout her time as Secretary of State, Hillary used her own private email account as opposed to only her government address, via a personal server which she has since wiped.

Among Hillary's initial justification for her actions was her assertion that she used the private account for convenience as she did not want to carry two devices. This was quickly scotched by the revelation that she uses multiple devices. Tripp for one is not surprised by the scandal that she has described as a 'timely and telling' indicator of Hillary's 'no rules apply to me' way of operating.

She explained: 'The scandals simply continue. She covers them up and moves on. People should be aware that she is probably the first cabinet secretary in the history of our country who has operated with their own private server, *for a reason*. Every lowly government employee understands that electronic communication on government-operated computers belongs to the United States.

'Hillary knows this and it's why she chose to break the rules. Because every document written on a government device is a record and it is retrievable forever more. Hillary's voluminous documents are not retrievable. She is answerable to no-one.'

She continued: 'She was clearly not answerable to the president for whom she worked and more importantly by actions she took, she was not answerable to the American public. 'She hands over what she chooses, deletes the rest and wipes the server clean. That is Hillary Clinton in a nutshell.'

Hillary Clinton Exposed, Movie She Banned From Theaters Full
Mars Daniels
2 years ago • 103,910 views
For more information, please visit: http://www.youtube.com/user/GLOBALPOLITICALAWAKE ...

We do not believe that violence against women is 'simply cultural'—we believe it is simply criminal ... I am proud that my [rapist] husband has stood up as President to confront the violence and to protect American women.

– Hillary Clinton, October 20, 1997

Hillary Clinton is a "feminist" because she has two things ... 1) female DNA that designates her body, anyway, as female, and 2) loyalty to the "anything goes, no taboos" non-ethic. As you will see with Beyoncé, "feminism" now means that the nothing-is-taboo non-ethic has to be embraced. We will meet the criminal Hillary a few more times in this series. She had sex with slave Cathy O'Brien and liked the mutilation she saw. [43] Cathy's credibility on this is backed up by her court documents in her second must-read book, *Access Denied For Reasons of National Security*. I always send blessings to Cathy and her family.

Must read: *Trance-Formation of America: The true life story of a CIA Mind Control Slave*

and *Access Denied: The documented journey from CIA mind control slave to U.S. Government whistleblower*

Both by Cathy O'Brien and Mark Phillips

To right, just two of the many documented proofs of Hillary Clinton's lying. Top, lying in sworn testimony, lower, a $35,000 fine for illegal campaign work. One of Hillary's critics is radio host Rush Limbaugh, and he was attacked by CIA Steinem and Fonda. Limbaugh is trying to expose Hillary Clinton. Apparently the CIA doesn't want her exposed. Forget democracy, think CIA.

Hillary showed disdain for non-career women when she said "I suppose I could have stayed home and baked cookies and had teas, but what I decided to do was to fulfill my profession, which I entered before husband was in public life." Does the reader hear her disdain? Let's review a bit about the Rhodes Scholarship and when Bill Clinton really entered public life.

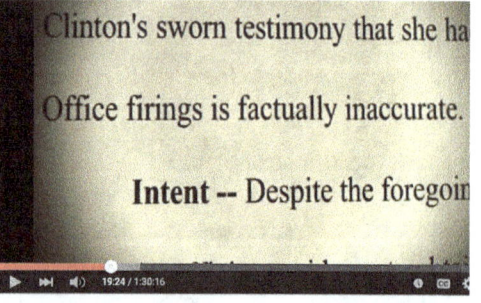

Hillary Clinton Exposed, Movie She Banned From Theaters Full Movie

The vaunted Rhodes Scholarship which Bill Clinton did not complete, like the Noble Prizes (Vol. 2, Chapter 8), is a fixed game show. There is nothing scholastic about it. It is about control. Cecil Rhodes was so deranged that he had a country named after himself, Rhodesia. He actually wanted the entire African continent to be under British rule. Just think how insane that is. He made his money from diamond mines, that were taken from the Dutch settlers with concentration camps in the Boer Wars which we will return to when we examine Gandhi, Vol. 2. Nathan Rothschild funded Rhodes until Rhodes controlled all the world's diamond mines.

Rhodes' biographer Sarah Millin noted, "The government of the world was Rhodes' simple desire." Said Rhodes, "The only thing feasible to carry out this idea is *a secret society gradually absorbing the wealth of the world,* to be devoted to this object." He was talking about his sponsors, the Rothschilds, who also sponsored Rockefeller in that same era. He was not postulating, he was promoting the already existent Illuminati banksters. According to Rhodes' own criteria, the traits most desired [For Rhodies] were [and are] "smugness, brutality, unctuous rectitude, and tact." [44] Does that sound like Bill Clinton?

Cecil Rhodes wrote several wills. His seventh and last will, named Nathan Rothschild administrator of his estate. It just means that Rothschild told Rhodes to give his money back. The will also established the educational grant known as the Rhodes Scholarships at Oxford University (which was controlled by the Fabians). [45] Who does the reader think controlled the Fabians? Of course, the Rothschilds! Please remember the name Fabians when we examine the Gay Movement, Vol. 2, Chapter 10. Rhodes had no wife or children. [46] He had crushes on men.

Author Roger Morris was an aide to Kissinger at the National Security Council until 1970, when he resigned over the bombing of Cambodia. According Morris' book *Partners in Power,* Bill Clinton was corresponding with Richard Stearns in 1969. According to Rampart magazine article 1967, the National Students Union (NSA, not to be confused with National Security Agency) was CIA sponsored, and Richard Stearns was international vice president. At this time Bill Clinton was trying to get out of the draft to go to Vietnam …

> "As international vice president [of NSA], Stearns almost certainly was witting [aware of] of the connection with the CIA: most of the CIA money was spent on the NSA's *international* activities. While at the NSA in December 1966, Stearns wrote to the UAW to propose a "program of aid conducted by American labor and students, for students in Spain working for the restoration of democratic government." This would have involved CIA funds from the NSA's International Commission, which was headed by Stearns. The international activities of U.S. labor were also CIA-funded at the time.

> "At a window of opportunity in the middle of Clinton's draft problems, we have him in a close relationship with Stearns at Oxford. Stearns had all the CIA connections anyone would have needed at that time, and the CIA was in the habit of securing exemptions for its assets. In a summer 1969 meeting with Willard Hawkins, the Selective Service head in Arkansas, Clinton agreed to "serve his country in another capacity later on" if the July 28 induction order could be lifted…"

> "… In 1970-1972, Stearns played a major role in placing Clinton in the McGovern campaign, thereby nurturing Clinton's political ambitions. Today Stearns is a judge in Boston. [From CIA to judiciary] Before Louis Freeh was selected, Stearns was considered by the White House as a possible appointee to head the FBI. [!]

> "[Author] Morris includes a chapter on Clinton's cooperation with drug-running and money-laundering operations at Mena, Arkansas during the 1980s. If Clinton was recruited by the CIA at Oxford, it explains why he would tolerate a CIA laundry in Arkansas—he was already compromised by his past association. [And he made fortunes.]
>
> "Ambitious young men don't "just say no" when the CIA comes calling. The CIA knows how to plant stories, spin the media, and set up scandals that can sink a candidate. Just ask Gary Hart, a 1988 candidate who for thirteen years had questioned the official version of the Kennedy assassination. Hart's presidential campaign was instantly derailed by the Donna Rice affair. In 1992, Clinton had a more serious bimbo problem than Hart ever had, *but it never became a media issue.*" [47]

So let's look at Hillary Clinton's statement again.

"I suppose I could have stayed home and baked cookies and had teas, but what I decided to do was to fulfill my profession, which I entered before my husband was in public life."

Does she mean when he was elected, or when they were living together in 1970 and he had already been in contact with CIA Stearn, who arranged meeting with HEAD of draft board? He was already on the political train. And the fact that Bill met a bisexual like Hillary, who amazingly could care less that he was a serial rapist, and that she herself then got into satanic abuse later on, would indicate that she also was "guided" in her perversions and trained. They were put together. It is too much of a coincidence that this match made in hell was a random meeting.

We are told that at age 15 Hillary Clinton met Martin Luther King, but Hillary has never peeped about the government assassination of King. [48] We are told she was president of Republican Club in early college and supported Goldwater, and then meets "community organizer" Saul Alinksy in 1968 and writes her senior thesis about his methods.

In Alinsky's 1971 book *Rules for Radicals* he wrote, "Lest we forget at least an over-the-shoulder acknowledgment to the very first radical: from all our legends, mythology, and history... the first radical known to man who rebelled against the establishment and did it so effectively that he at least won his own kingdom — Lucifer."

We are told she met Alinsky several times and corresponded. We are told that her 1969 commencement speech at Welsey college along with her photo was printed in *Life Magazine!* Someone was putting her on a fast track! We are told she had high profile jobs like working on Black Panther case. Like Bill, Hillary was groomed very early for political life. By whom!

"Hillary interned [as an attorney] with the Edelman's Children's Defense Fund after graduating from law school in 1973, and Edelman became her trusted friend and mentor ..." Her own website says summer of 1970. I wonder why the discrepancy? In the coming election, some feel that women will vote for Hillary as irrationally as Blacks voted for CIA Obama. Will you?

> "Among recent secretaries of state, Hillary Clinton was one of the most aggressive global cheerleaders for American companies, pushing governments to sign deals and change policies to the advantage of corporate giants such as General Electric Co., Exxon Mobil Corp., Microsoft Corp. and Boeing Co.

*"Instead of doing much to try to protect their citizens from Fukushima, Japan, the U.S. and the EU all just raised the radiation levels they deem "safe." Nuclear expert Arnie Gundersen says that high-level friends in the State Department told him that **Hillary Clinton signed a pact with her counterpart in Japan agreeing that the U.S. will continue buying seafood from Japan, despite that food not being tested for radioactive materials.*** [49]

"At the same time, those companies were among the many that gave to the Clinton family's global foundation set up by her husband, former President Bill Clinton. At least 60 companies that lobbied the State Department during her tenure donated a total of more than $26 million to the Clinton Foundation, according to a Wall Street Journal analysis of public and foundation disclosures.

"Mrs. Clinton's connections to the companies don't end there. As secretary of state, she created 15 public-private partnerships coordinated by the State Department, and at least 25 companies contributed to those partnerships. She also sought corporate donations for another charity she co-founded, a nonprofit **women's group** called Vital Voices…

"… The foundation resumed soliciting foreign governments after Mrs. Clinton left the State Department. The official name of the foundation was changed to the Bill, Hillary & Chelsea Clinton Foundation. Mrs. Clinton became a director. All told, the Clinton Foundation and its affiliates **have collected donations and pledges from all sources of more than $1.6 billion,** according to their tax returns. On Thursday, the foundation said that if Mrs. Clinton runs for president, it would consider whether to continue accepting foreign-government contributions as part of an internal policy review."

– Zerohedge.com Feb 21, 2015

From Alinsky's claims to work for the underdog to collecting money from the largest "have" companies in the world, and creating "vital women's voices" to vote for her, who or what is Hillary Clinton other than just another perverted political *puppet*?

"… I want to be that champion. You don't have to get by. You can get ahead, and stay ahead."

The entire idea of "progress" is a ponzi scheme. Until we hear leaders talk of zero growth and cleaning up the mess, the mess will get worse. Instead of getting ahead, we need to come clean and plan for the future of the next generation, not ourselves. Then we will put something before our own *disconnecting vanity,* we will put compassion and sacrifice where it should be, on the altars of our own selves.

Beyoncé Knowles

Singer Beyoncé Knowles is married to a satanist named Jay-Z who appears to be her handler. She was given to him by her former handler, her father.

In images below we see Jay-Z's clothing line with the motto used by arch satanist and bi-sexual Aleister Crowley, followed by Beyonce's modesty destroying 2014 Grammy Awards presentation, and to top it off, an image that I hope will insult your sensibilities, her "Feminist" VMA (MTV Video Movie Awards) choreography, which she neither created nor understands.

"Do what thou wilt" in images below means there are NO MORAL STANDARDS. Do whatever you want. Anything goes. DE-moralized. No morals. You are the master of your destiny. Me me me me. There is no accountability. "Do what thou wilt!" I think Aleister Crowley's favorite song went like this … Me me me, me me me, me me me … On the way he got syphilis.

The old school feminists resented being sex objects. The new "feminists" are just sex objects. They are on a mission to destroy modesty and innocence, and teach girls that their only worth is as spread legs. We are being conditioned to this new normal. This is called "trans-formation," with bill board staging proclaiming that a card carrying satanist slut role model is a "feminist."

I hope by now that the reader would not be surprised that CIA *Ms. Magazine* would promote a spread leg satanist like Beyoncé Knowles. The headline says "Beyoncé's Fierce Feminism." The word fierce comes from Beyoncé's album "Sasha Fierce" the alter ego that many feel is an actual demonic entity that possesses her. Image to right from her "I am Sasha Fierce" album clearly shows the goat symbol (twice) of the Illuminati satanists.

Katy Perry left,   Gaga above.

Madonna, Spears, Aguilera, Cyrus, Prince William Illuminati satanic Baphomet Goat <> devil's horns. Those who are most willing, become engaged in ritual heinous crimes to prove their loyalty, seal their silence, and win position. For Prince William see excellent DVD The Zion King or on Youtube.

Feminist? What is the message from Beyoncé and CIA *Ms. Magazine*? Wearing satanic symbolism is fashionable? Being used for sex is feminism? Hello? Talk about a puppet on a string. This is first time I saw high heels having a practical use. Exemplary? Beyoncé was forced as a little girl to drink the kool aid and CIA *Ms. Magazine* wants you to also. A psy-op must contain something true, so while promoting a satanic puppet, CIA *Ms. Magazine* includes health and fracking on cover to suck in reader, just as the natural history portion of the Kratts brothers' cartoon show sucks in kids. The reader of CIA *Ms Magazine* is tricked and then exposed to the subliminal message that someone as distorted as Beyoncé could somehow be normal, acceptable, laudable, a leader. Is she? For you? You can jump way ahead, as I won't cover Beyoncé further until Vol. 3, and please go on internet and listen to this youtube below. This is list of links to study. [50]

Secrets of Magic and Mind Control - feat. Beyonce & Jay Z
by Freeman Fly
3 months ago • 55,126 views
Move over Madonna, there's a new High Priestess in town and her name Considering that **Beyonce** was Time ...

HD

A May 2015 stage performance by Beyoncé's husband's buddy Pharrell Williams on The Voice. Pyramids are put in staging over and over again to push the trance. We have to have someone at top of pyramid controlling us, right?

1.3 billion people are told this in China, and the talent shows are telling us the same thing.

Beyoncé's satanist husband Jay-Z and Pharrell Williams to right, have a 1% worshipping clothing line called the "Billionaire's Boys Club," mentioned again in epilogue of Vol. 2. Photo to the right is Pharrell Williams with the all-seeing-eye of the pyramid of abuse, masqueraded as a peace sign on the blue hand and behind him. Big Brother will bring peace. Pharrell Williams is covered in Vol. 3 of this series and his job is to be a mannequin, wearing designer clothing for the distraction of the masses who are trying to "get ahead" while he wears slave chains of gold. Oprah Winfrey joins in this 1% worship, as we will see.

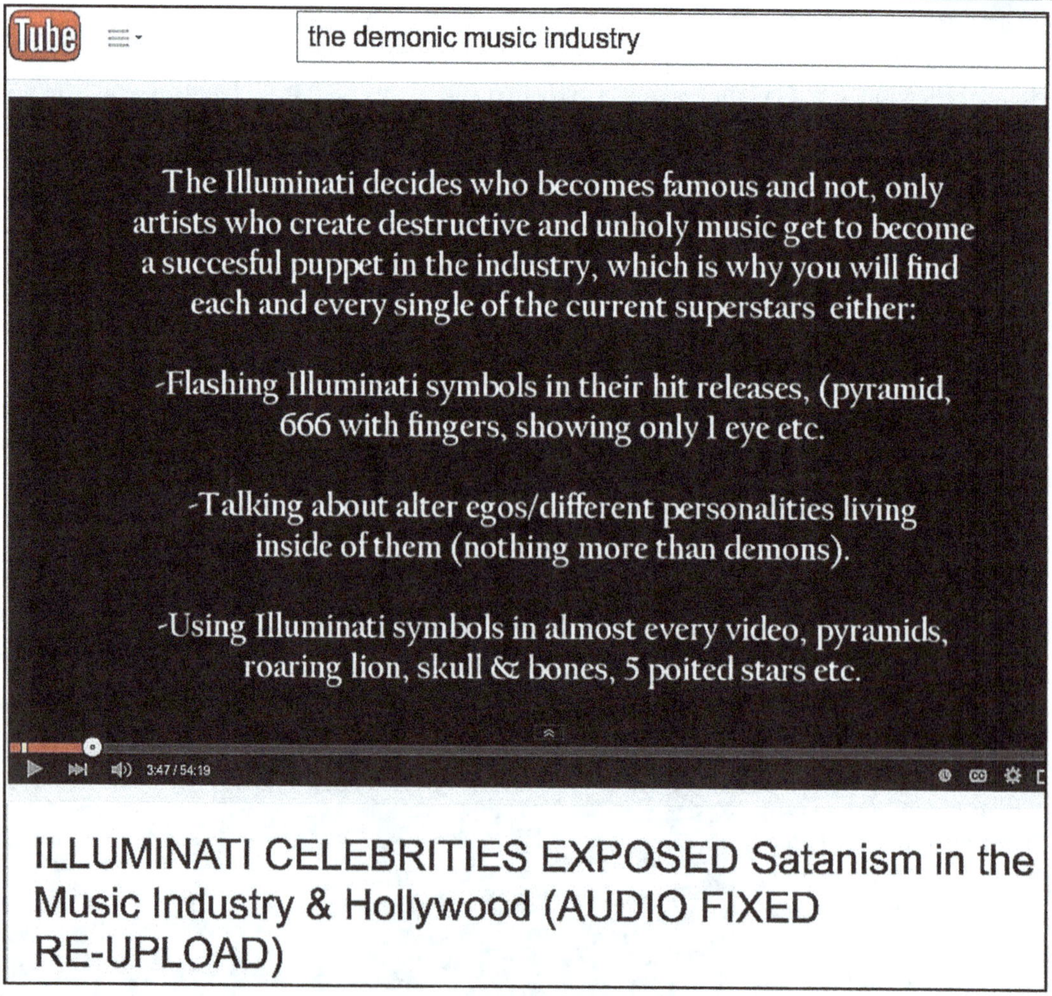

the demonic music industry

The Illuminati decides who becomes famous and not, only artists who create destructive and unholy music get to become a succesful puppet in the industry, which is why you will find each and every single of the current superstars either:

-Flashing Illuminati symbols in their hit releases, (pyramid, 666 with fingers, showing only 1 eye etc.

-Talking about alter egos/different personalities living inside of them (nothing more than demons).

-Using Illuminati symbols in almost every video, pyramids, roaring lion, skull & bones, 5 poited stars etc.

ILLUMINATI CELEBRITIES EXPOSED Satanism in the Music Industry & Hollywood (AUDIO FIXED RE-UPLOAD)

If talk of demonic spirits seems far fetched, you have either never read the Bible or any other scripture, or haven't traveled overseas where witchcraft, in its lethal reality, is still practiced. There is more to existence than meets the eye, and invisible things do exist, despite being invisible. Above a youtube by Thomas Warren Channel, and there are many other excellent researchers also. Some are Christian, some aren't. All agree, something evil is in our midst.

Let's call it what it should be called, evil *CIA Magazine*. Oh, the reader doesn't like the word evil? Too judgmental? But are you judging the word itself? There is NOTHING good about the CIA. Why did the Central Intelligence Agency create *Ms. CIA Magazine*? Why? Please keep asking that. This is a deprogramming book. We deprogram by asking questions and staying alert.

We are programmed to see things in an isolated way. We have determined that Steinem and *Ms.* are CIA. The CIA is evil without any question. Please go back to the genital mutilation in Chile with dogs and the CIA connections with that terrorism.

Now with our eyes on straight, we see *Ms. CIA* pushing actress Angelina Jolie, with her Zionist and globalist connections, [51] "taking on child marriage" (tiny byline). In other words, interfering with diverse cultures elsewhere, while *CIA Ms.* ignores child trafficking in U.S., thereby protecting it. [52] Below Jolie's *Malificent* movie (Sold at William Gates' Costco, June 2015) billboard, which cast a satanic goats-horn image (goat head ring of Beyoncé above) on whole cities for a film that was supposedly for children. In 2007 Jolie joined Council of Foreign Relations (CFR) created by the Roth-efellers. She officially touts "humanitarian" lies that Syria needs U.S. to intervene, when U.S. funded

genocide in Syria to begin with. [53] Jolie IS lipstick and war crimes. Bi-sexual Obama, bi-sexual Jolie. No clear polarity or morality. *Evil CIA Ms. Magazine.*

When we put our eyes on straight, what is Steinem–Beyoncé "Feminism?" How about the third cover in green? What happened to your "love life?" Gone. Now it is your sports sex life. Carnal, indulgent, distracting from *what is important which is becoming activists for purification.*

Let's put our eyes on straight. Why is a satanist like Jay-Z and his wife Beyoncé supporting CIA Obama? [I tagged his shirt.] Oh, that's right, the CIA and the satanists are both evil. Incidentally, Jay-Z shares his mind-programmed wife with other men, including, as announced and allowed on Twitter, CIA Obama. [54]

Have we seen "progress" under CIA Obama or have we seen him attack whistleblowers like Wikileaks Hero Julian Assange and NSA whistleblower, Hero Edward Snowden? Did we watch CIA Obama lie about Gaddafi attacking his own people, which never happened, and invade Libya and destroy it using hired "rebels" that were then exported to Syria to do the same thing? We did. [55] Did we watch CIA Obama send Hillary Clinton to Libya to speak with Gaddafi who came out of hiding in a caravan with white flags and was attacked and murdered, with a fake youtube immediately coming out, making it seem like a "lone gunman." We did. Did we hear Hillary Clinton cackle, "We came, we saw, he died." [56] We did.

Without Gaddafi's support, South Africa would still be under apartheid. He was a humanitarian hero, and simply because he was a good man who wanted liberation for Africa from outside hegemony, he was maligned and blamed for one fake terrorist attack after another. [57] Gaddafi was smeared as funding terrorists in Illuminati mind programming movie, *Patriot Games* (1992), with puppet Harrison Ford. Muammar Gaddafi was a great and good man who told the truth to the UN that the biggest terrorists in the world are the members of the UN "permanent" security council. The U.S./NATO bombing of Libya destroyed hospitals, schools, and their irrigation system. This was to save them of course. Do an image search for Gaddafi and what comes up are ugly images of him frowning or bleeding to death. You don't see the image to right, do you? That is *social engineering,* bending you. Google is part of the Beast.

Put it all together dear reader, the organized *social engineering* mobsters are going after your innocence and corrupting the *natural feminine* as fast as they can.

They are taking over other nations to steal resources.

They are crushing indigenous cultures everywhere, and horribly in Papua New Guinea.

Cyrus is Beyoncé is Steinem is MacLaine is Fonda is Clinton is Obama is Kissinger is Oprah. They support each other in a seamless circle of deception and acquisition and false pride glory.

So in order to unravel our confusion about gender or power or sex or self-esteem, we need to understand who is pulling the strings because our confusion was created. That is what this series is about ... Figuring out how to take back our power. Let's now wrap up this little book that is starting to immerse you into the plot of the series, with an interesting screen shot I took.

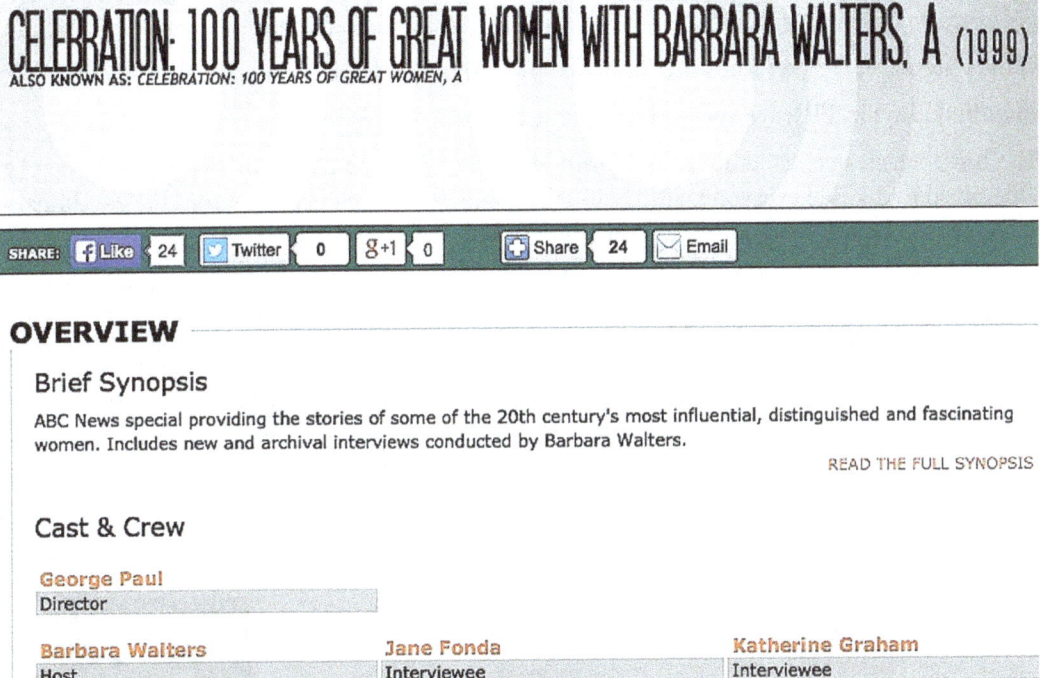

Barbara Walters is a network employee who interviews whoever the controlled media want her to promote or smear. She did not choose these "great" women. Walters would get fired if she revealed what is really going on behind the scenes. She knows this. She is complicit. She goes along with a dishonest job. She would be scared to death to be a whistle blower. Is anyone accountable?

Let's please review these supposedly "great women" and notice what they have in common.

Jane Fonda at this point in 1999 had done what to be one of the "Greatest Women?" The main thing she had done was being an actress and a fitness video producer. She was married to Tom Hayden (who is now controlled opposition writing ridiculous articles that Al Qaeda and ISIS [58] are *not* funded by U.S. and NATO) "Greatest woman" Fonda, after marrying a "radical" then married arch-establishment Ted Turner, who is an apologist for control freaks like David Rockefeller. This is her award for towing the line. Her undercover (pun intended) work may never be known. She may go to her death bed under mind control.

Katherine Graham (Jewish ethnicity will be examined later in Vol. 2, because there are some big questions) mentioned in story about CIA Steinem, ran the CIA *Washington Post*, and helped cover up what really happened when Henry Kissinger organized the Watergate Scandal to take down Nixon. (Nixon was placed by Nelson Rockefeller with condition of naming Kissinger as Secretary of State. Kissinger had worked for Nelson for 10 years. With Nixon out of White House, pedophile new President Gerald Ford, who used young child Cathy O'Brien, was ordered to make Nelson Rockefeller his Vice President. Nelson almost got his dream, but news of an affair he had had, ended his very long plan to be President. Nelson Rockefeller was of course under orders also.) So, what was great about Katherine Graham? She ran a New World Order CIA propaganda publication just like Steinem! As I said, awards are about cementing the program.

Gloria Steinem, well, we know her now. She may go to her death bed under mind control.

Elizabeth Taylor. I'll leave you with the quote below.

The last interviewee listed above is **Oprah Winfrey** who was placed as part of the New Age Operation to distract everyone with "self-help" while she herself is part of the elite psychopaths that needs to be exposed. See next screen shot of internet search.

So what we behold with the above "Great Distinguished Women" in 1999 is that they were all decadent puppets for the machine, and it is the machine that spreads the machine's message by making the puppets seem important.

Why was the meeting below secret? Keep asking that. So I guess Oprah's real reasons for being named the "greatest" is a secret, since we don't really know what she is about. But we do know. She is a puppet in the same group that Cecil Rhodes mentioned …

"The only thing feasible to carry out this idea [of one world government] is a secret society gradually absorbing the wealth of the world."

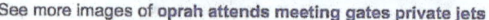

Lipstick and War Crimes

"*Get drunk, put on your mask and pull your false self together.*"

The story of Oprah's lavish girl's school in South Africa, which purposely selected many girls without parents, is telling. "Diamonds and dreams." It is an ivy league school for "leaders" to mold Africa HER way, the elite way. (Remember, Winfrey was sexually programmed from age 9. She is an agent. She was promoted and placed before us, just like Hillary Clinton. Winfrey was given the role in lesbian CIA Alice Walker's movie *The Color Purple.* Placed. Black men decried the movie as extremely sexist, which it was. The movie's heroine lesbian scene featured a liberated prostitute. Get it? Sensualism will never help the world.)

Oprah's South African girls' school ... "Winfrey said she got resistance from the very beginning, even from the school's architects.

"The resistance was too much," Winfrey said. "'What are you doing? What do they need all that room for? Why does a girl need all that closet space when she has no clothes?' That's what they first said to me." [Winfrey couldn't understand that people don't need a lot of clothes. In her elite bubble the architects seemed "too much."] "And my idea was to understand, yes, you come from nothing, but oh, what a something you will become, if given the opportunity," Winfrey said ... [With opportunity you too can have a lot of clothes and a big closet to hide your covert life.]

"Diamonds and Dreams: Winfrey, who will stay very involved with the school and even teach leadership classes, said she believed the future was unimaginably bright [rich like her, going to secret meetings, being the 1%] for all of the girls. 'Somebody asked me, what do I think will happen or what do I imagine for them. I don't. I don't imagine. ... I can't imagine what it's like to have a miracle like this. It's just a miracle,' Winfrey said."

[She thinks unsustainable material wealth, a model of disparity, is a miracle. And that, of course, makes her, *in her own eyes,* a miracle worker!

Amazingly, she earned none of her money, just as Bill Gates or Katherine Hepburn earned none. All of these sponsored puppets simply did as they were commanded, and were paid to obey. Example is attending the secret meeting. The more they obey, the more ego candy and wealth they are given because they are stable in their programming and don't let their conscience question the pyramid of abuse.

In the elite insanity, Winfrey feels she is a miracle worker to corrupt young girls with luxurious promises of hoarding success, when her own money came from just being a puppet.

Winfrey spent $40 million on one decadent school for the elite entitled female hoarding CEO's of the future, when she could have built 100 schools to teach tens of thousands of kids sustainable skills and values. She pushes elite/slavery hierarchy on fellow black people! How many slaves does it take to hold up the Billionaire Girl's Club of South Africa?]

"... Winfrey dressed up for the school's opening ceremony, diamonds and all. The girls had seen them in pictures, and Winfrey said she had worn them as a signal that this was an important celebration." [She felt it important to dangle the carrot before them.] [59]

> *"And all of it came into absolute, explosive, joyous fruition on the day we went shopping at Bed, Bath and Beyond."* - Oprah Winfrey October 12, 2012

Oprah is just another New World Order recruiter. Oprah goes from New Age self-help to diamonds. Gaga goes from flesh to Diamonds (Vol. 2, Chapter 8). Same outcome. (Song "Diamonds are Forever" in Vol. 3)

I would like the reader to know, that I was perfectly startled to find out that ALL of the women featured in this book were and are covert programmed agents being used to "transform" us for the New World Order. And all were or are sexually dysfunctional. I thought they were just egotistic celebrities, but I discovered they were all groomed agents/slaves from an early age. All the famous/rewarded male agents/slaves are the same. It is time to clean the kitchen.

The Intelligent Student's Guide to the New World Order

www.conspiracyarchive.com/NWO/Intelligent_Students_NWO.htm

– By Erica Carle

What is the New World Order?

The essence of the New World Order (NWO) or world management system is that it is management by social engineers, rather than government based on a written constitution. How you are affected by this management system depends on what the social engineers decide the system should do for you and require of you. The social engineers and system managers think of themselves as scientists applying the scientific method to the control of group behavior. Your behavior and your relationships are regarded as the subject of investigation and control by those who call themselves social scientists. You are among their test animals, and you have no say in, and often no knowledge of, experiments that involve you. If the NWO is totally implemented, your independence, individuality, and freedom will be gone.

There is nothing new about the idea of managing others, or even of controlling the whole world. That has been the goal of social philosophers for thousands of years. However, we need not go back over ancient history. We are concerned primarily with what has been going on in our own generations. This we can understand quite well if we confine ourselves to the Nineteenth and Twentieth Centuries.

Goals of the New World Order

To begin to understand the New World Order (NWO) you need to forget what you have been told about philosophical differences between Republicans and Democrats; left and right; Socialists and Libertarians; business and labor; liberal and conservative; black and white, etc.. The planners of the New World Order know they must use, influence, and cater to all of these groups to accomplish the goals they are seeking, which are:

1. Consolidate everything.
2. Commercialize everything.
3. Classify everything.
4. Claim everything.
5. Control everything.

Every one who we think of as famous was placed by a corrupt system. Now below are some women who should be much better known, because they are against corruption.

Some Truly Great Women

If you are reading this as a paper back book, you can find this list with live links at www.Lipstick-and-war-crimes.org in Free section.

- Cathy O'Brien: Hero mind control sex slave survivor and whistleblower, author of *Trance-formation of American* and *Access Denied for Reasons of National Security*

- Brice Taylor: Hero mind control presidential model survivor. Author of *Thanks for the Memories.*

  "This amazing autobiographical account of Brice Taylor's personal experience, reveals the hidden purpose behind the ritual abuse and mind control that is being reported around the world! It shares her recollections of being conditioned through childhood in order to be used by Bob Hope and *Henry Kissinger*, as a mind-controlled slave into adulthood … and used as a presidential sex toy and personal "mind file" computer by high ranking individuals around the world to further the agenda of the New World Order. This book will help you navigate your way through the treacherous times we now face in the 21st Century."

- Cisco Wheeler: Hero mind control survivor, author of *Behold a White Horse*

- Karen Wetmore: Hero mind control survivor, author of *Surviving Evil: CIA Mind Control Experiments in Vermont*

- Elisa E: Hero mind control survivor, author of *Our Life Beyond MK-Ultra.*

- Journalist Sharon Attkisson: busted CDC for making up false numbers about the fake Swine Flu "pandemic." (Robert Kennedy Jr.'s 2014 book *Thimerosal: Let the Science Speak* affirms this CDC corruption.)

- Leuren Moret: continues to connect dots between environmental pollution and secret agendas.

- Dr. Judy Wood: 9/11 researcher wrote *Where Did The Towers Go?*

- Cynthia McKinney: hopefully will be our first woman President, didn't bite the bait while in Congress about 9/11, and witnessed Israeli blockade of medical supplies to Gaza first hand, among much other hero activism. www.allthingscynthiamckinney.com

- Dr. Vandana Shiva: Seed, GMO and women's right activist India. www.navdanya.org

- Bethany Hamilton: lost her arm to a shark but continues as champion surfer athlete and Christian leader. www.Bethanyhamilton.com

- Nomi Carmona: GMO and transparency activist in Hawaii. www.babesagainstbiotech.org and https://www.facebook.com/BabesAgainstBiotech

- Deborah Dupre: Independent journalist covered Blue Plague after Gulf Oil Spill-Gusher, and the subject of Targeted Individuals. See http://deborahdupre.com

Deborah was a caretaker of my house, and a day before her arrival someone entered the room where she would be staying, and propped a lamp behind the door, so when I went to open it to see if it was clean, the door bumped the lamp, and I had to reach around to move it. I remember feeling groggy that morning. She absolutely is targeted, and now myself, 5 years later, am also. The surveillance state knows which bedroom I am sleeping in, though I have no cell phone, or smart meter, and leaves messages like bent forks or holes in the wall, to spook me. Deborah has experienced much worse. Why? She is a whistleblower. The most anti whistleblower administration ever has been Obama's.

- Regina Meredith: Conscious Media Network

- Catherine Austin Fitts: Former U.S. Assistant Federal Housing, connects the dots, see her website Solari Report.

- Benedictine Sister Tresa Forcades: helped expose the fake Swine Flu and who was behind it. Just do search for her name.

- Jane Burgermeister: vaccine/eugenics awareness activist from Austria, see www.birdflu666.wordpress.com

- Carolyn Baker: website Speaking Truth to Power www.carolynbaker.net/

- Daw Aung San Suu Kyi: Burmese human rights activist

- State Senator Nancy Shaefer: murdered for revealing child trafficking by the Child Protection Service. See youtubes.

- Singer Lauryn Hill: challenging the music industry.

- Angela Davis: prison whistleblower and black community healer www.davisangela.com/

- Bonnie Faulkner: independent radio journalist, 'Guns and Butter' KPFA Podcast.

- Rigoberta Menchu: Mayan survivor of CIA funded ethnic cleansing in Guatemala and human rights champion.

- Cindy Sheehan: Iraq war protestor.

- Rosalind Peterson: geo-engineering/chem-trail coverup. http://www.agriculturedefensecoalition.org

- Ina Gaskin: book *Spiritual Midwifery* and more.

- Charlotte Iserbyt: public school dumbing down whistleblower. http://deliberatedumbingdown.com/

- Dolores Huerta: United Farm Workers of America

- Beverly Eckert: assassinated for standing up to 911 Commission. "My silence cannot be bought."

- Kerry Cassidy: black ops and secret tech whistleblower/investigator, www.projectcamelot-portal.com

- Christina Hoff Sommers: fake-feminism whistle blower, wrote *Who Stole Feminism?* and *The WAR AGAINST BOYS: How Misguided Feminism Is Harming Our Young Men*

- Faith Morgan: The Power of Community video.

- Kay Baxter: Seed and Self Sufficiency pioneer from New Zealand

- Naomi Klein: book *Shock Doctrine. CIA Ms. Magazine* did honor her in 2001.

- Jessica Lynch: Blew whistle on fake coverage of her abduction experience in Iraq.

- Kelly Dougherty and Maggie Martin: Iraq and Afghanistan Veterans Against the www.ivaw.org (not to be confused with war crime enabling iava.org)

- Elana Freeland: author of *Sub Rosa America* series and *Chemtrails, HAARP, and the Full Spectrum Dominance of Planet Earth*

- Helena Norberg-Hodge: Founder of Local Futures/International Society for Ecology and Culture, www.localfutures.org

- Deborah Tavares: StoptheCrime.net

Anuradha Mittal: Stealing Nature

* * *

And as a last positive note, I would like to honor the 557 school principals in New York State who stood up like responsible Mama Bears against the Gates Foundation "Common Core Curriculum" foisted on all U.S. Schools. (Image page 52) This curriculum is planned to go global, with one curriculum methodology for the entire planet if the World Bank has it's way. (*Lipstick and War Crimes: Vol. 3*). This is globalization info you didn't get in school.

The NY Principals' April 21, 2014 statement can be found here.

http://scfeeney.files.wordpress.com/2014/04/anopenlettertonewyorkparents_21apr14.pdf

Common Core Curriculum was sold to states with monetary incentives by CIA Obama and the eugenics Bill and Melinda Gates Foundation. The purpose is to increasingly disallow teachers and schools to have individual styles. The curriculum further quantifies learning in order to take another step in dumbing down society. My daughter this year brought home a one page summary of Martin Luther King that gave the false reasons for his death, and specifically emphasized that he was killed by one man, which was disproven in censored 1999 court trial. [60] Common Core will insure that all students are given standardized propaganda and that students who can learn like robots will excel and be placed for management positions in the future. Ipads for early grade school are used to track not only aptitude, but personality, and create data base on children. "The Achievement Gap is Widening" means that a psychological profile is pre-chosen for leadership. Leadership means servitude to the "outcome based" culture.

Thank you, Principals of New York State, for your resistance!

* * *

The information in the series will be compelling and perhaps, profoundly upsetting. As Debbie Lee said, "The narratives in our heads are not ours!" It has been said that before the truth sets you free, it will piss you off.

That is healthy! Be angry, not DE-moralized.

As a warning, you may find yourself denying, bargaining, and going through all Elizabeth Kubler-Ross' "Stages of Grief," until you die to the programming and come to accept … that what I and so many others have presented is not opinions, but is simply real evidence. Some readers may be blown away already. Did some priests and priestesses get de-frocked for you?

So chin up, we have a lot of digging to do.

We will study together and go further into symptoms, causes and solutions. By the way, I'm not trying to sell books, I'm trying to blow a whistle. I'm hoping there will be money to pay for more whistles. If you find this information valuable, it is important that you help spread it. We need millions of whistle blowers now. Please start to include education in your social contacts. The survival of your friends and family is literally in your hands.

Please understand that the most criminally insane people in the world are in control of Hollywood and Wall Street and the Pentagon and Congress and the Supreme Court and the White

House and Google and Facebook and the major foundations and corporations. The pyramid of control has it's hand on all these levers of society. The entire scientific community is as controlled as Big Media. [61] You will have the evidence to decide if this might be true by the end of the series. This pyramid of abuse runs drugs protected by U.S. military in Afghanistan, they traffic women and children (which means sex slavery until the victims are killed, which is why the bondage images of the Divas are so heinous), they run profit from war and run pedophile rings [62], and they sacrifice human beings, mostly children, in secret ritualistic initiations. I'm sorry to shock you, but this is the real world. I've known about this for a couple years but I still find it hard to accept. Power is wielded through silence forged on terror. We have to expose these people.

If you are a woman reading this, you and I are of different genders, but that makes no difference in our dedication to virtue. Our ability to be humane has nothing to do with gender. I say that with the utmost sincerity.

For any women out there that think men cannot be trusted, consider the journalism of Keith Harmon Snow and this article supporting women against rapist pedophile men, and a system which traffics children taken into custody by the state.

http://www.consciousbeingalliance.com/2012/05/a-life-sentence-family-courts-sacrificing-mothers-and-children-in-america/

So now, Christians and non-Christians, you don't have to be suspicious of me because of my church affiliations or lack of, you need to be suspicious of everything you are told on TV and in your newspapers. We all need to be suspicious of new laws that take away our rights for our "safety," like mandatory vaccines for children in school. Whenever we see a global trend, we need to take sides *against* monoculture. I love Mama Bear. I encourage all men and women to become courageous Mama Bears and protect this Earth by *standing up for virtue* in all places. Virtue does not impose on others, yet standing up against imposition is important. Rather than "my rights," or the rights of my tribe or creed, we need to embrace the rights of future generations to be free of a machine. We don't think like this enough, but the heroes I list above, show us the way. I believe the state and it's *social engineering* programs are our common oppressor. De-centralization, purification, rejuvenation … The ancient is our road forward.

– Ray Songtree, September 2015

The many mini essays that define the glossary terms below, can be found at the end of Vol. 2 or can be downloaded free as pdf at www.lipstick-and-war-crimes.org.

Index of Glossary and Central Concepts

1. Cage theme
2. Compassion
3. Consumerism
4. Controlled media
5. Co-opt
6. Cutout
7. "Democracy"
8. "Developed" countries
9. "Developing" countries
10. Disconnecting vanity
11. Dominant culture
12. Doublespeak
13. Entitled
14. Evil
15. "Freedom"
16. Globalists
17. Globalization
18. Grasping desire
19. The Great Mystery
20. Hero
21. His-story
22. Indigenous people
23. Informed choice
24. Inverse relationships
25. Military
26. Monoculture or monopolization
27. Personal sovereignty
28. Predictive programming
29. "Progress"
30. Purification path
31. Recovering from "development" countries
32. Re-localization
33. Resource depletion
34. Roth-efellers
35. Rothschild
36. Sanctioned disease
37. Social engineering
38. Technocracy
39. Transparency
40. Unsustainable
41. Urban people
42. Vanity

Endnotes Trailer

Lipstick and War Crimes: Vol.1

1. Interview with *USS Liberty* Survivor Richard Larry Weaver
   https://lipstick-and-war-crimes.org/1967-uss-liberty-attacked-by-submarine-uss-amberjack-crew-member-blows-whistle/

2. Soviet KGB defector Yuri Bezmenov
   http://www.illuminati-news.com/2007/0714a.htm

3. Terrorist zionists before World War II.
   http://guardian.150m.com/palestine/jewish-terrorism.htm

4. Francis Bacon, author of the King James Bible
   http://www.hiddenmysteries.org/religion/christianity/bacon.shtml

5. Club of Rome quote from "The First Global Revolution," a Report by the Council of the Club of Rome by Alexander King and Bertrand Schneider 1991. This led to the Rio Summit, and UN Agenda 21 which maps out depopulation goals and complete land usage plan for entire world

6. NASA letter blasting Global Warming as poor science
   http://climatism.wordpress.com/2014/02/02/former-nasa-scientists-reject-global-warming-crisis/
   http://www.inquisitr.com/1234575/nasa-scientist-global-warming-is-nonsense/

7. Peer review questions
   http://www.healthmlmscam.com/pubmed-impact-factor-peer-review-journals-and-fraud/

8. Radiation in San Diego, California
   http://www.godlikeproductions.com/forum1/message1426090/pg1

9. HAARP and Geo-engineering—Just search those words, lots of information.

10. 2001 Navy plans for ice free arctic
    www.star.nesdis.noaa.gov/.../2007IceSymp/FinalArcticReport_2001.pdf

11. Bohemian Grove – Just search those words, lots of information.

12. Bengladesh War Crimes against women
    http://www.nytimes.com/2010/08/25/world/asia/25iht-letter.html?_r=0

13. Use of pornographic movies in institutional rape in 1971 Bangladesh
    www.womenundersiegeproject.org/conflicts/profile/bangladesh

14. Increase of sexual violence in military
    http://www.csmonitor.com/USA/Military/2014/0505/Sexual-assault-in-the-military-What-happens-when-the-victim-is-a-man-video
    http://rt.com/usa/sexual-assault-military-increase-899/
    www.wnd.com/2013/05/military-suffers-wave-of-gay-sex-assaults
    http://www.adn.com/article/20140505/sexual-assault-military-what-happens-when-victim-man

15. IMF austerity measures
    http://www.xat.org/xat/worldbank.html

http://www.unitypublishing.com/Government/IMF.htm

16. Various

    http://bfeldman68.blogspot.com/2007/08/ms-magazines-restricted-archives-part-1.html

    Gloria Steinem: How the CIA Used Feminism to Destabilize Society By Henry Makow Ph.D. 2002

    Black Feminism, The Cia And Gloria Steinem. [2003]
    http://whale.to/b/how7.html

    [video] Gloria Steinem Exposed: Feminist Spy for The CIA!

    Black Feminism, The Cia and Gloria Steinem. (Fwd: For You That Blames Black Men For Everything.)
    http://www.newswithviews.com/NWO/newworld22.htm

    Book, *The World Split Open: How the Modern Women's Movement Changed America* – Ruth Rosen.

17. 1999 Shelby Tennessee trial exonerates James Earl Ray

    https://lipstick-and-war-crimes.org/hiding-the-verdict-the-1999-martin-luther-king-civil-trial/

18. Kissinger war Crimes Laos and Cambodia

    www.thirdworldtraveler.com/American_Empire/Nixon_Cambodia_LFE.html

    VIDEO Cambodia www.youtube.com/watch?v=KOcRlEHrGBU
    www.historycommons.org/context.jsp?item=cambodia_655

19. Agent Orange Kissinger

    http://www.agentorangerecord.com/home/
    http://www.codepink.org/attempting_citizens_arrest_of_henry_kissinger_for_war_crimes
    www.march-against-monsanto.com/agent-orange

20. Oprah Winfreys molested as child

    http://www.dailymail.co.uk/tvshowbiz/article-2239102/Oprah-Winfrey-opens-traumatic-childhood-David-Letterman-lecture-series.html
    http://www.dailymail.co.uk/tvshowbiz/article-1265591/Kitty-Kelley-discovers-identity-Oprah-Winfreys-real-father—doesnt-know.html
    http://www.sheknows.com/entertainment/articles/807417/shocking-oprah-winfrey-drug-allegations
    http://www.imdb.com/name/nm0001856/bio
    http://www.kazantoday.com/WeeklyArticles/oprah-winfrey.html

21. Beyoncé Knowles pregnant age 14 from controlled home. That doesn't add up. Who was father?

    http://www.celebuzz.com/2013-05-16/a-20-minute-conversation-with-beyonces-uncle-larry/
    https://www.youtube.com/watch?v=hnEwGrJ_QlU

22. Hugh Heffner *Playboy* CIA

    40% of A. C. Spectorsky's first 15 authors who were promoted on *Playboy's* cover were British or American intelligence agents/assets.

    http://anolen.com/tag/mr-playboy-hugh-hefner-and-the-american-dream/

    "Hugh Hefner's *Playboy* Enterprises, like the other fronts which banked with Castle Bank & Trust of Nassau, is a CIA-sponsored business concern."

    http://anolen.com/2015/02/10/do-you-have-a-key-to-the-playboy-mansion/

    Playboy and the (Homo) Sexual Revolution. November 9, 2001 by Henry Makow Ph.D.

    "Thus "sworn enemies," *Playboy* and feminists, found common ground in hatred of healthy heterosexuality expressed in the nuclear family. As a result of the (homo)sexual revolution, society now suffers from epidemics of family breakdown, pornography, impotence, child sexual abuse, sadosexual violence, teen pregnancy, a cocktail of STD's and, of course, AIDS. The birthrate has

plummeted by 60% since 1960 and is now below replacement level. But we must not stand in the way of social progress."
    www.henrymakow.com/091101.html#sthash.3TBCbxwD.dpuf

23. Jane Fonda military parents, goes to Vietnam 1972
    http://academics.wellesley.edu/Polisci/wj/Vietimages/fonda.htm

24. Kissinger links
    http://www.bilderberg.org/kissing.htm
    www.expertbear.com/kissinger-war-crimes
    www.wariscrime.com/new/the-case-of-kissinger

excerpt from book *The Trial of Henry Kissinger,* by Christopher Hitchens.
    http://www.counterpunch.org/2002/04/28/henry-kissinger-wanted-man/

Do search Kissinger Pedophile and Kissinger Mind control

25. Obama family members in Kenya question his blood relation
    http://aangirfan.blogspot.com/2012/06/real-obama.html
    http://www.infowars.com/obama-disowned-by-african-half-brother/

26. The movie, "Dreams of My Real Father" by Joel Gilbert
    www.obamasrealfather.com

In my opinion the movie explores Obama's history without connecting some dots. For example, Gilbert portrays teenage Anne Dunham, Obama's mother, as running away and having sex with Davis. There is no way CIA Stanley Dunham had a daughter that was not under CIA surveillance and therefore control. Gilbert didn't get into the fact that the 1960's Weatherman and Symbionese Liberation Army were CIA front groups,
    (http://www.maebrussell.com/Mae%20Brussell%20Articles/Why%20Was%20Hearst%20Kidnapped%201.html).

Gilbert portrays Davis as a communist insider, but Davis was under FBI surveillance for 19 years and very well known, as was Bill Ayers. As was Saul Alinsky. I believe all these change agents were covertly supported in order to bring about the "transformation" of the American system, just as the Bolsheviks were created in New York City, to "transform" the Russian system. The method of the New World Order's destabilization and consolidation is the foundation of Vol. 2 of this series. Consider that the FBI had completely infiltrated the Black Panthers. If they could do that, then they infiltrated or created other groups also. Consider that both Hillary Clinton and Barack Obama were involved with Alinsky. The FBI and CIA knew all that. These associations were all tracked and supported.

Perhaps, like myself, Gilbert didn't want to confuse the viewer with the subject of false flag attacks and double agents too early in the exposé of our New World Order fabricated matrix of lies. "The individual is handicapped by coming face to face with a conspiracy so monstrous he cannot believe it exists." - FBI J. Edgar Hoover .

Frank Marshall Davis's entire sanctioned career (why wasn't he harassed or assassinated by FBI like Malcolm X and Martin Luther King and the Black Panthers) and his association with Stanley Dunham was all tracked by CIA, meaning Frank Marshall Davis, even if he wasn't employed by CIA as I feel he was, and sent to stir up trouble in Hawaii (which is the method of Hegelian Dialectic explored in Vol. 2, funding both sides of a conflict), he was under 19 years of surveillance. Therefore his sexual escapades with teenage Anne were known by FBI and CIA, period. I say CIA agent Stanley Dunham was ordered to give his daughter to Davis for beta-kitten programming as she definitely had a CIA career, and therefore, Davis was a CIA sanctioned trainer and handler. The photos of Anne Dunham show beta kitten programming, not just nudity. The purpose of such photo shoots combined with sex for young girls is to destroy inhibitions. This is boot camp for female CIA agents. We see the same pattern over and over. In exact same way Shirley MacClaine's CIA father gave Shirley to mind control programming, as did Cathy O'Brien's father, as did John Hinckley's father (1981 attempted assassination of Reagan by Bush Sr. using son of Bush's friend, Vol. 2.)

Still, *Dreams of My Real Father* is a must see movie. It is pity that it is not free yet. Because there is so much disinformation in the form of partial truths, I have to ask myself if Gilbert was allowed to produce a movie that was not as insightful as it could have been, but then, people could say that about me also. In the movie, Obama is shown being chummy with Muammar Gaddafi and Hugo Chavez as some kind of indication that Obama was supportive of bad men. Gilbert may not understand both were very good men, and that both were murdered under the Obama administration to take over Libya and Venezuela, which were standing up to New World Order hegemony because of their courageous leaders. More in Vol. 2. Perhaps Gilbert can produce a sequel.

I recommend this article on Obama.
http://www.thecommonsenseshow.com/2013/09/22/the-cia-manchurian-candidate-groomed-by-communists-to-destroy-america/

This article however, doesn't seem to mention that Communism was a Rothschild Illuminati production. (Vol. 2) These are all opposing factions created to "transform" the ancient through "change" and "progress."

27. Amnesty International on dogs used to mutilate women in Chile
    http://beyondweird.com/conspiracy/cn09-31.html

28. Black male voice on book *Black Macho* and Michele Wallace
    http://www.topix.com/forum/afam/TJGOOJ66D6DGJLOKB

29. U.S. history with Indonesia military
    http://www.hrw.org/news/2010/07/22/indonesia-us-resumes-military-assistance-abusive-force
    http://westpapuamedia.info/tag/us-military-aid/
    http://awpasydneynews.blogspot.com/2012/09/1-concern-that-us-military-aid-to.html

    China involved also
    http://www.radionz.co.nz/international/pacific-news/210446/chinese-military-aid-to-png-for-troop-carriers,-armoured-cars-and-uniforms

    and Australia
    http://hrlc.org.au/australian-government-urged-to-adopt-human-rights-safeguards-in-military-aid-programs-as-west-papua-marks-anniversary-of-indonesian-control/

30. Henry Makow summary of *Spin Sisters*
    http://rense.com/general75/how.htm

31. Study on young women's career objectives
    http://www.historylearningsite.co.uk/feminism_education.htm

32. Mind Control, Presidential models
    http://www.wanttoknow.info/mindcontrol
    http://vigilantcitizen.com/vigilantreport/the-hidden-life-of-marilyn-monroe-the-original-hollywood-mind-control-slave-part-ii/

33. Marilyn Monroe's slave past
    http://aangirfan.blogspot.com/2008/02/marilyn-monroe-and-cia.html
    http://vigilantcitizen.com/vigilantreport/the-hidden-life-of-marilyn-monroe-the-original-hollywood-mind-control-slave-part-i/

34. Nazi roots of mind control
    https://www.bing.com/search?q=mind+control+nazi+experiments&qs=n&form=QBRE&pq=mind+control+nazi+experiments&sc=0-20&sp=-1&sk=&cvid=78a1a2516a254fe2b7f4249945b7fcfe

35. The real Earth Day founder Ira Einhorn in jail on false charges.
    http://www.angelfire.com/on/GEAR2000/declaration.html

36. Charlie Sheen attacked for questioning 9/11

    His video is worth seeing
    https://www.youtube.com/watch?v=ZyKR2-A0KPU
    https://www.youtube.com/watch?v=CY4lsrrelU8
    http://www.prisonplanet.com/articles/march2006/220306mediablackout.htm

37. Hillary bisexual
    https://www.bing.com/search?q=hillary+bisexual&pc=MOZI&form=MOZSBR

38. Hillary abuse of Cathy O'Brien

    Search for book Trance-formation of America by Cathy O'Brien online.

39. Bill Clinton serial rapist
    https://www.bing.com/search?q=bill+clinton+serial+rapist&pc=MOZI&form=MOZSBR

40. Bill Clinton drug lord
    http://www.theforbiddenknowledge.com/hardtruth/the_crimes_of_mena.htm

41. Suspicious deaths surrounding the Clintons
    http://whatreallyhappened.com/RANCHO/POLITICS/BODIES.html

42. What really happened at Waco
    http://www.carolmoore.net/waco/

43. Judy Gibbs killed and Gary Johnson almost killed.
    http://rcjustice.tripod.com/pres.html

44. Ibid 37

45. Cecil Rhodes quotes
    http://www.theforbiddenknowledge.com/hardtruth/reviewing_rhodes.htm

46. Rhodes Scholarships controlled by Fabians
    http://modernhistoryproject.org/mhp?Article=FinalWarning&C=5.1

47. Ibid 44

48. Bill Clinton CIA early connections
    www.oocities.org/capitolhill/8425/CLIN-CIA.HTM

49. Ibid 16

50. Hillary Clinton signs deal to continue importing radioactive food from Japan
    http://www.washingtonsblog.com/2012/03/california-slammed-with-fukushima-radiation.html
    http://solarimg.org/?p=1722

51. Beyoncé links—watch this entire series. They don't connect the dots, they leave that to you. You will have to watch it more than once, and study some mind control videos also. Search *satanic Beyoncé*. All these people are slaves. Beyonce starts in Part 2 of youtube series. In Part 3 notice how familiar she is with Obamas. Intimate. Cage Theme is discussed in Vol. 3.
    https://www.youtube.com/watch?v=sj-VkExyfsQ

    Hip Hop
    https://www.youtube.com/watch?v=hnEwGrJ_QlU
    https://www.youtube.com/watch?v=pVjgNcftfgQ
    https://www.youtube.com/watch?v=pVjgNcftfgQ
    http://abcnews.go.com/International/beyonce-jay-zs-trip-cuba-legal-treasury-department/story?id=18920026
    http://vigilantcitizen.com/latestnews/roseanne-barr-mk-ultra-mind-control-rules-in-hollywood/

52. Angelina Jolie Zionist and Globalist links
    http://www.helpfreetheearth.com/news644_angelina.html

53. Jolie calls for intervention in Syria, history of U.S. in Syria
    http://asheepnomore.net/2015/04/27/cfr-angelina-jolie-calls-for-war-with-syria-at-the-united-nations/
    http://empirestrikesblack.com/2012/02/angelina-jolie-conscripted-to-sell-genocidal-humanitarian-intervention-war-doctrine/

54. The Economics of Child Abduction - David Shurter
    https://lipstick-and-war-crimes.org/the-economics-of-child-abduction-and-the-elite-david-shurter/

55. Jay-Z, R Kelly, Beyoncé 3-way
    http://diaryofahollywoodstreetking.com/jayz-r-kelly-beyonce-sitting-in-a-tree/

    Beyoncé with Obama, and Michelle, lesbian, transvesite?

    First … study all the discrepancies in Obama's story. This article is well referenced.
    http://www.deflationeconomy.com/obama-cia-agent.html
    http://www.infowars.com/breaking-smoking-gun-evidence-obama-born-in-kenya/

    Obama admits Frank Marshall Davis connection – film Dreams of My REAL Father – by Joel Gilbert
    https://www.youtube.com/watch?v=D47i8VsNYgo

    Trailer of movie
    https://www.youtube.com/watch?v=UMUlWbO1rhk

    Beyoncé as presidential model. Watch Beyonce intimate kiss with the President of United States and Michelle
    Minute 7:25 https://www.youtube.com/watch?v=9ruSI-skk_Y

"He seems to have a heterosexual marriage, but there are rumors that Michelle was a militant lesbian at Princeton. Then there's Larry Sinclair's book and videos, saying Larry had sex with Obama on specific dates, twice, while Obama provided cocaine, once at a hotel and another in a taxi. One date fits with a date that Obama was not present in the state legislature. Another odd detail is that Obama's faculty counselor at Occidental College in LA was gay, and was generally the gay counselor for gay students. Was Obama one of those gay students? or an exception? Did Obama ever date any woman prior to marrying Michelle? He seems to have no interest in women, until meeting the lesbian Michelle. They have a marriage of convenience, for Obama's political goals. Single people are at a major handicap in politics. They need the pictures of a loving family, heterosexual family and children, to get votes in America. Is Obama gay? Is he avoiding being too favorable in gay issues such as don't ask, don't tell, in order to hide his gay life? Never dated women through his teens and early twenties? How did he manage that?"

"Larry Sinclair also says he knows some distinguishing characteristics of Obama's private parts, as proof. Larry Sinclair gave a press conference, but was arrested a year ago, last June, by a warrant obtained by Joe Biden's son.

"There is a retired restaurant owner in Chicago who had gay customers. She says they said Obama was gay. Obama attended Trinity Church of Christ, which had a gay choir director, a good friend of Obama, the gay choir director was murdered, when he tried to contact Larry Sinclair."
    http://www.topix.com/forum/topstories/TP26BBE988TL9UBQT/p3

    Transgender Michelle?
    https://bobbiblogger.wordpress.com/2008/11/27/michelle-obama-the-day-she-learned-she-couldnt-have-it-all/

    The reader can assess whether the next link has any merit.
    http://beforeitsnews.com/obama/2014/03/irrefutable-proof-that-michelle-obama-is-a-man-247-2461574.html

56. NATO rebels used in Libya then sent to Syria to fake as rebels
    http://globalresearch.ca/search?q=HISTORY+SYRIA&x=0&y=0
    http://www.globalresearch.ca/libyan-terrorists-are-invading-syria/32358
    http://www.globalresearch.ca/british-sas-special-forces-dressed-up-as-isis-rebels-fighting-assad-in-syria/5466944

57. Hillary reaction to Gaddafi death
    http://www.globalresearch.ca/search?q=HILLARY+DEATH+GADDAFI&x=0&y=0

58. Fake terror attacks blamed on Libya
    https://www.bing.com/search?q=lockerbie+false+flag&qs=HS&pq=l&sc=8-1&sp=1&cvid=701e827bf4bf435e9af90a003d702b51&FORM=QBRE
    http://www.globalresearch.ca/the-biggest-secret-in-history-false-flag-terror/5441247

    Libya falsely framed for terrorist attacks

    German TV exposes CIA, Mossad links to 1986 Berlin disco bombing
    http://100777.com/node/101
    http://www.globalresearch.ca/propaganda-alert-the-lockerbie-bombing-who-was-behind-it-libya-iran-or-the-cia/5373053
    http://rehmat1.com/2009/08/23/lockerbie-was-mossad-false-flag-operation/
    http://www.independent.co.uk/news/uk/politics/lockerbie-evidence-planted-by-cia-1586487.html

59. Hayden articles do not name U.S. backing of Alqueda and ISIS

    "The apparent "defeat" of that al-Qaeda by the U.S. and the tribes spawned a splinter insurgency, which has become ISIS in Iraq."
    http://tomhayden.com/home/avoid-splinters-in-iraq-syria.html

    compared to the truth
    https://www.bing.com/search?q=Mossad+Isis&pc=MOZI&form=MOZSBR

60. Oprah Winfrey's elite mind control girl's school
    abcnews.go.com/GMA/story?id=2767103&page=1

61. Ibid 16

62. Scientific data controlled by 6 corporations
    http://www.naturalnews.com/050457_science_publishing_academic_oligarchy_corporate_corruption.html

63. War used to collect children for pedophile rings
    https://lipstick-and-war-crimes.org/how-power-is-controlled-dr-sue-arrigo-sex-slave-survivor-details-how-cia-uses-war-zones-to-harvest-children-and-sex-for-blackmail/

64. See Vol. 2

65. World Trade Center 7
    www.youtube.com/watch?v=Zv7BImVvEyk

66. Search "danger mercury in tuna study"

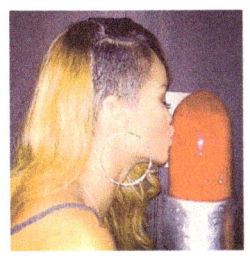

Table of Contents

for Lipstick and War Crimes: Vol 2

(Cast of Characters)

Rihanna, "Diva" of seductive materialism

War Criminal Henry Kissinger

Introduction   1

David Menongye – Hopi | Kobun Chino Roshi – Zen Master | Steve Jobs | John and Mina Lansa – Hopi | Thomas Banyacya – Hopi | David Holmgren – Permaculture | *YouTube – The Disclosure Project Press Conference, May 2001* | *YouTube – 9/11 Loose Change* | David Icke | Yolngu People – Arnhemland, Northern Territories, Australia | Song – "This Land is Your Land" by Woodie Guthrie | *Youtube – Operation Deep Forest* –NSA attack on Maori in New Zealand | David Wilcock | Movie – *Elisyium* (2013) – Matt Damon | song "I'm Yours" by Jason Mraz | Glossary terms summary

Chapter 1   Organized Consumerism 15

Movie – *Finding Nemo* (2003) | Song – "I Get Out" – Lauryn Hill | Movie – *Captain America* (2014) – Robert Redford | Ralph Nader | "Logo" Barack Hussein Obama | Movie – *Brave* (2012) – Disney/Pixar in Mandarin | The Peace Corp | Graeme Wearden – *Guardian* | George Soros | Albert Einstein | Normon Dodd – 1954 Congressional Committee | Rockefeller, Guggenheim, and Carnegie Foundations | George Bernays, Father of Public Relations | Using crisis | George Bush Sr. (George Herbert Walker Bush) – Pedophile (U.S. spelling) and War Criminal | Iranian Prime Minster Mosaddeq killed – 1953 CIA Operation Ajax – overthrow of | Iran's democratically elected government | Shah of Iran | Ayatollah Khomeini | Osama bin Laden | Alice Bailey – "New World Order" – 1918 | UN Lucis Trust – (formally Lucifer Publishing) | Erica Carle – *The Intelligent Student's Guide to the New World Order* | Education 2000 | Naomi Klein – Author *Shock Doctrine* | J.P. Morgan – *Rothschild* Bankster | *Cutout* Winston Churchill | Jon Christian Ryter – Researcher | *Cutout* FDR – Franklin Delano Roosevelt | Senator Claremont Pell – Earthquake Weapons 1976 | HAARP (High Frequency Active Auroral Research Program) | Goldman Sachs Inc. | C. Edward Griffin – FED *Hero* Whistleblower | AMA – American Medical Association | FBI Chief Ted Gunderson – exposes rampant child sacrifice for satanic rituals – | Gunderson was murdered with arsenic | Henry Kissinger – Pedophile and War Criminal | Robert McNamara – Viet Nam era war criminal becomes President World Bank | Zbigniew Brzezinski – author of *Between Two Ages: America's Role in the Technetronic Era* | *Cutout* Bill Gates – On trial in India,

2014, for vaccine crimes | Prince Philip | Donald Rumsfeld | Leuren Moret – *Hero* Whistleblower | FEMA – Federal Emergency Management Agency (Creates and manages emergencies) | Johann Adam Weishaupt – Founder of Illuminati 1776 | *Virtue* by author

Chapter 2   All the Man's Kings 41

Amschel Rothschild – Father of Modern Banking Andrew Hitchcock – Rothschild *Hero* Whistleblower The *Rothschild* Timeline | George Washington Henry Jackson Benjamin Franklin | Nathan Mayer Rothschild – England Jacob (James) Mayer Rothschild – France Prince William IX of Hesse-Hanau | East India Company | Napoleon Bonaparte | Wellington – Battle of Waterloo | Thomas Jefferson | Kalmann (Carl) Mayer Rothschild pals with Pope Gregory XVI | Karen Hudes – World Bank Whistleblower | Guiseppe Mazzini – Illuminati agent | Jack Ruby – Paid assassin of Oswald | Lee Harvey Oswald – Framed | John C. Calhoun – Vice President under Andrew Jackson | Jacob Schiff – Foremost Rothschild agent in U.S. Founded FED, ADL, NAACP, and | Bolshevik Revolution | British Prime Minister Benjamin Disraeli | Cherokee and Creek Native Americans – Trail of Tears | Karl Marx – Rothschild Employee | Karl Ritter – Anti-thesis of Communist Manifesto | Friedrich Wilhelm Nietzsche | Abraham Lincoln | Tsar Alexander II – Rothschild enemy | John D. Rockefeller – Standard Oil funded by Rothschilds | Frederick Engels | David Allen Rivera – Author | Warren Buffet | *Cutout* Arnold Schwarzenegger | The FED – Federal Reserve a private Rothschild bank that refuses to be audited | ADL – Anti Defamation League | James Earl Ray – Exonerated in (censored by Media) 1999 trial, Shelby Tennessee. Did not kill Martin Luther King. | NAACP – National Association for the Advancement of Colored People | Collin Powell – War Criminal | Condoleezza Rice – War Criminal | *Cutout* Oprah Winfrey | *Sellout* Jessie Jackson | Eddie Murphy – Owned | Cynthia McKinney – *Hero* Whistleblower | Movie – *The Monuments Men (2014)* directed by George Clooney | Jesus | Buddhism

Chapter 3   The Mask Comes Off 61

Paul A. Volker – *Roth-efeller* minion The Bilderberg Group for real Edmond de Rothschild | Sharon Percy Rockefeller | Andrew Gavin Marshall – Researcher | Pawns in a Game | *Cutout* Vladimir Lenin | *Cutout* Adolf Hitler | *Compromised* Mahatma Gandhi *Compromised* Woodrow Wilson *Cutout* Chairman Mao | *Cutout* Stalin *Cutout* Bill Clinton *Cutout* George Bush Jr. | Color Revolutions and Arab Spring | Salvador Allende – Chile – Murdered by Kissinger | Operation Condor – South America – Kissinger | Bill Van Auken – Researcher | John Kennedy Jr. – murdered 1999 | Yom Kipper War – 1973 – a la Bilderberg Group | UN Agenda 21 – You are to live in a Smart City where you will be happy. | *Compromised* Dalai Lama | Song "If I Ain't Got You" by Alicia Keys | Vandana Shiva – *Hero* GMO, Seed, Women's activist India | Chinese environmental activists | Walmart | WTO World Trade Organizations | IMF – International Monetary Fund (Noose) | Nelson Mandela | Ryan Shapiro – Researcher | Hermann Kallenbach – Gandhi's handler | Gopal Krishna Gokhale – Gandhi's mentor | Joseph Lelyveld – New World Order minion | Bob Marley – Artist, song writer, truther

IMAGES FROM LIPSTICK AND WAR CRIMES: VOLUME 2

Chapter 4   Entitlement, The Bad Boy 75

Cutout Australian Prime Minister Paul Keating | *Cutout* Australian Prime Minister John Howard | Martyr Senator Paul Wellstone – another airplane crash | Fake Swine Flu – practice for false flag Ebola | Sharyl Attkinson – *Hero* Journalist | CDC – Center of Disease Control (Controlling the Dissemination of Cancer and other diseases) | RFID chips | More Lipstick Please: George Orwell | Urban Blight | Noam Chomsky | Song "Ramona" by Bob Dylan | Sir Baldwin Spencer – Snob explorer aboriginal communities | Palestinian Children Killed | Emperor Nero | Geo-engineering – Weather modification plus ionizing atmosphere for other programs

Chapter 5   Freedom for the Rich 93

Chapter 6   The Ocean Is Broken 95

Greg Ray – Sailor | Plankton Decline – Not discussed | Geo-engineering | Global Dimming | Elana Freeland – author of *Chemtrails, HAARP, and the Full Spectrum Dominance of Planet Earth* | Dead Fish | Dane Wigington – *Hero* Whistleblower GeoEngineeringWatch.org | Vincent Freeman – Nanotechnology Whistleblower | Transhumanist Agenda | *"If it's covered up, it's true."* – Chuck Cannon, San Francisco | Autism graph | Alzheimer's graph | Prostate Cancer UK graph | Hepatitis C, UK graph | NAS Graph Tennessee | Food Stamp – Ration Graph | Soil Erosion Graph – We inherit reality, we don't create our own reality. | Water per Capita Graph | Cell Tower/ Electro Sensitive Graph | Sanctioned Diseases | Bertrand Russel | Fluoride | USAF Major George R. Jordon – Fluoride | Mike Adams – *Hero* Whistleblower – NaturalNews.com | Mercury | EMF Pollution – Electro Smog | "Smart" Meters | Dirty Electricity – Switching Mode Power Supply | Josh del Sol – *Hero* Whistleblower – Producer of film *Take Back Your Power* | Breast Cancer | FCC – Intentionally obsolete safety standards | Bioinitiative.org – Thousands of studies show long term danger of wifi | Five Danish Ninth Grade School Girls – *Hero* Whistleblowers | Another Fake Pandemic | Gary Null and Richard Gale – *Hero* CDC Whistleblowers | No Ebola epidemic, case numbers disappearing in Liberia | Dave Hodges – CDC and Bill Gates own patents on Ebola | Monsanto Inc. | Ebola Vaccine impossibly produced in a few months | Bioweapons Lab at epicenter of Ebola in Sierra Leone | Jane Burgermeister – Vaccine Agenda *Hero* Whistleblower | The Bill Gates You Should Really Know | Email by Author | Bill and Melinda Gates – The rich will manage us for our own good and make sure we want it. | Gates – Global Food Supply | Gates – Geo-engineering | Gates – Vaccine Deaths | Gates – Trial in India names Gates | Kenya WHO sterilization campaign | "Depopulation Vaccine" in Kenya and Beyond by *Hero* journalist Jon Rappoport

Chapter 7   Just Look In the Mirror. 159

song "Man in the Mirror," sung by Michael Jackson | Concept *Disconnecting vanity* | Movie *Brave* (2012) in Spanish | song "A Thousand Years" by Christina Perri | Patrick Henry | Furor David Rockefeller | Richard Henry Pratt – Carlisle Indian

School | General Philip Sheridan | Denise Oliver Velez – American *Indigenous Hero* Whistleblower | The Disney Weapon | Gloria Steinem – CIA agent | song "Can't Hold Us Down," by Disney brat Christina Aguilera | song "Stand By Your Man" by Tammy Wynette and Billy Sherrill | The 1970s Illuminati ISIS | Madonna | Cher | song "Stronger Than Me" by Amy Winehouse | Katherine Hepburn – promoted by Howard Hughes | Lady Gaga | Unregulated cosmetics | song "Once in a Lifetime" by Talking Heads | Prostituting Ourselves | Selling Disconnection | song "From This Moment" by Shania Twain | song "Danny's Song" by Kenny Loggins | Take a Good Look at My Face | song "Take a Look at My Face," Smokey Robinson | Gay – origins of word | King Louis XIV – "L'etat cc'est moi" (I am the state) (and King of Fashion) | Breast feeding or fetish? | Michelle Obama | Women join the battle front

Chapter 8   Shamelessness and the All-Seeing-Eye 195

"Ella" – 17 year old talent show contestant | *American Idol, X-Factor, The Voice* | Simon Cowell – Freemason | Reinhard Mohn – Nazi heir, controls X-Factor | Demi Lovato – Disney brat | Selena Gomez – Disney brat | MK-ULTRA mind programming | Tim Olstad – talent show contestant | King Frederick William I – Prussian compulsory schools | The Disney Machine | Miley Cyrus / Hannah Montana | Ted Schwarz – Author *Secret Weapon* | Katy Perry – Another music industry *cutout* | Britney Spears | Christina Aguilera | Someone is Watching | George Washington | Warren Buffet | Madonna and Spears/Aguilera | Madonna and Cyrus | Charlie Chaplin | Trans-humanism | Hillary Clinton – Lesbian/Bi-sexual | Posers as Teachers | Jennifer Lopez | The Zionist music industry | E. Michael Jones culturewars.com | Larsha Moon on Mass Enslavement through Sex | song "Live It Up" by Jennifer Lopez, Britain's Got Talent 2013 | Gag Order | Lady Gaga | Elton John | Disney Inc. | Walt Disney – another *cutout* | Fritz Springmeier – Author of *The 13 Illuminati Bloodlines* | Robert Kennedy Jr. on families | song "Born This Way" by Gaga | song "Alive" sung by Dami Im | Queenie | Maltese Cross | Queen Elizabeth | song "God Save the Queen" by The Sex Pistols | Knights of Malta and Sovereign *Military* Order of Malta | Rothschilds | Shakira – another "diva" Illuminati *cutout* | Adolf Hitler | Benjamin Disraeli | "Sir" Norman Schwarzkopf | "Sir" Collin Powell | Madeleine Albright | "Sir" Henry Pedophile Kissinger | "Sir" Brent Scowcroft | "Sir" Alan Greenspan | "Sir" George Pedophile Herbert Walker Bush and "Sir" Ronald Reagan | "Sir" J. Edgar Hoover | "Sir" Tom Jones | "Sir" Mick Jagger | Freemasons | Rihanna | Celine Dion | New Age Movement | Deepak Chopra | Image – The California drought | Movie – *Why Are They Spraying* (2012)

Chapter 9   In Your Own Home 245

Video Games | Sesame Street / Muppets / Disney | Gaga and Elton John | Nicki "Three Way" Minaj | song "Roman Holiday" by Nicki Minaj | Whitney Houston – Sacrificed | Aguilera and Minaj | Sam Bailey – Winner UK *X-Factor* talent show 2013 | *Cage Theme* | Alex and Sierra – Winners USA *X-Factor* talent show 2013 | Khloe Kardashian | Taylor Swift

**Chapter 10   Is the Gay Movement Another New World Order Social
               Engineering Project?. 260**

Marshall Kirk – Blueprint for Gay movement | Dr. William Thetford, CIA – A Course in Miracles | Adam Lambert | Katy Perry | George Washington | Carrie Underwood | Ellen Degeneres | Talent show judges | Elton John | Melanie Amaro | Kylie | Rudolf Giuliani | Gordon Brown | Fabians | Princess Diana | Jayz and Aleister Crowley | Anderson Cooper | Texe Marrs Whistleblower | Rabbi David Saperstein | Rabbi David Eidensohn | Eretz Israel | Will Smith and children | The Economics of Happiness |

Glossary   265

Endnotes   287

Coming up Images from
Lipstick and War Crimes Volume 2 and 3

by Ray Songtree

"Sir" Tom Jones   Demi Lovato   Jennifer Lopez   Adam Lambert   Simon Cowell

Will I Am   Brittany Spears   Randy Jackson   Jessie J   Nicki Minaj

Harry Connick   Pharrell Williams   Kylie Minogue   Keith Urban   Usher

X-Factor, The Voice, Idol Judges are ALL Illuminati puppets. The all-seeing-eye of slavery.

        949,657 Total views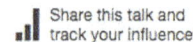

In her talk, Melinda Gates makes a provocative case for nonprofits taking a cue from corporations such as Coca-Cola, whose plugged-in, global network of marketers and distributors ensures that every remote village wants — and can get — a Coke. Why shouldn't this work for condoms, sanitation, vaccinations too? (Filmed at TEDxChange.)

Interactive transcript

Melinda Gates
Philanthropist

Melinda French Gates is co-chair of the Bill & Melinda Gates Foundation, where she puts into practice the idea that every life has equal value. **Full bio**

"It is likely that the Bill and Melinda Gates Foundation will continue its commitment to global population control, and now, curriculum creation in the nation's schools because they truly believe that they know better than anyone else how we all should live."

– Anne Hendershott (Chapter 6)

Fake blonde Shakira with all-seeing-eye claims 70 million facebook followers. Do they know she is a slave selling them materialism and sex object conditioning? Vol. 3.

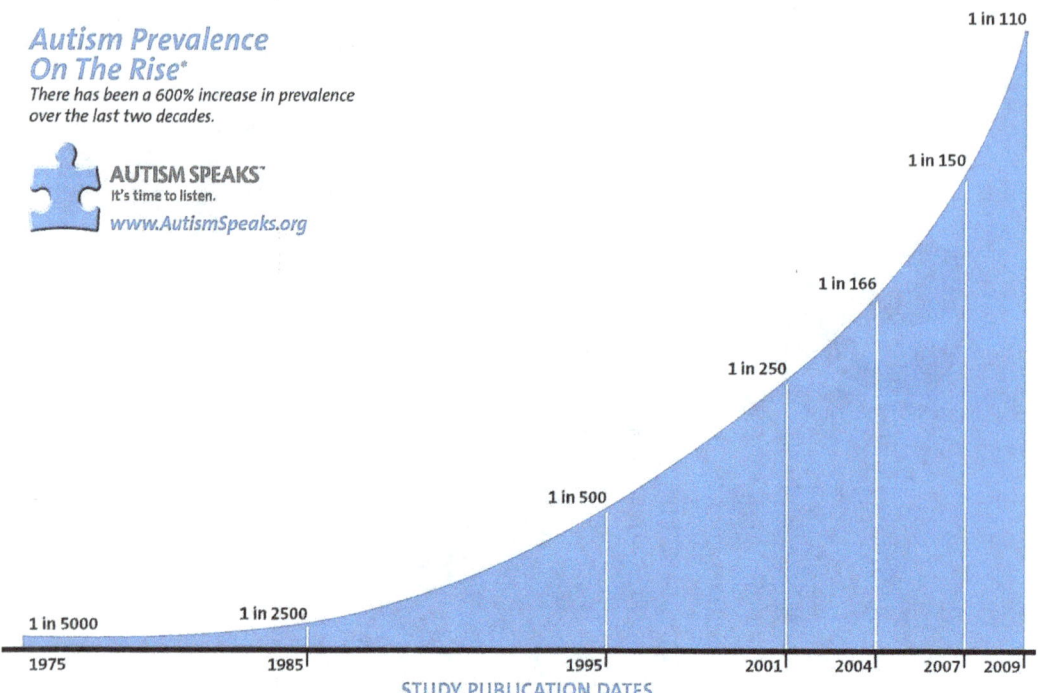

Robert Kennedy Jr. has helped write a 2014 book, *Thimerosal: Let the Science Speak* about mercury based thimerosal, which is still in flu vaccines. The connection with Autism is absolute. He exposes the CDC for what it is. A cover up agency. In a speech on April 7, 2015 he states …

"All the things that are supposed to stand between rapacious industry and our little children have been dismantled, all those checks and balances, the press, the politicians, the regulatory agencies, the courts, they are all gone. And the only thing left is the parents. And now they are trying to get rid of them."

– Congressman Robert F. Kennedy Jr.

June 19, 2015: Rutherford, N.C., Jeff Bradstreet, Doctor and Pastor, who linked autism with vaccines was found dead in river with gun shot wounds to chest. "Multiple law enforcement officials said the U.S. Food and Drug Administration searched Bradstreet Wellness Center last week." Dr. Bradstreet had treated 1,100 cancer patients with immune system booster GcMAF, with 85 percent response rate.

One of his supporters wrote … "He did NOT kill himself! He was murdered for who he was speaking against, what he knew, and what he was doing about it. He was brilliant kind compassionate doctor with amazing abilities to heal. He was taken. Stopped. Silenced. Why would a doctor who had access to pharmaceuticals and could die peacefully shoot himself in the chest???? And throw himself in a river?? THIS IS OBVIOUS! MURDER!!"

At home and globally, we build collaborative partnerships with those who share our mission. By matching vital educational needs to our partners' goals, we create real impact together.

"Our continued collaboration provides an opportunity to positively impact early childhood on a global scale with the latest technology."

Kristin Parsley Atkins, Senior Director, Wireless Reach, Qualcomm

USA, Sesame Street

> learn more

"What helps make our Grow Up Great program so effective is the association we established with Sesame Workshop from the beginning. Our collaboration has created an innovative partnership that continues to encourage early learning."

Eva Tansky Blum, Senior Vice President & Director Community Affairs, PNC Bank Chair and President, The PNC Foundation

USA, Sesame Street

Doctors warn of breast-cancer link to keeping cell phone in bra

  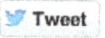 

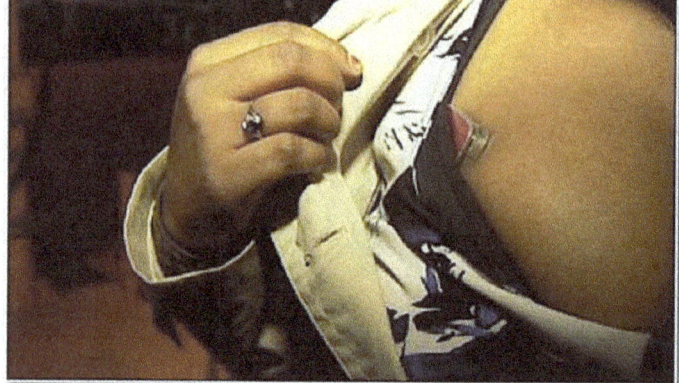

Cell phone bra breast cancer link special report

KTVU.com

OAKLAND, Calif. — Could where you carry your cell phone make you sick? Some doctors say they're seeing evidence of breast cancer that could be linked to where some women keep their mobile phones.

Tiffany Frantz and other young women tell KTVU it's convenient way to hold on to their cell phone. "I put my cellphone right in my bra," said Frantz.

Related

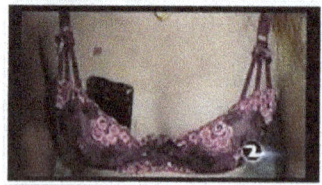

SPECIAL REPORT: Keeping cell phone in bra may lead to breast cancer

Carefully hidden fine print warnings endanger public, but protect FCC and tech corporations from lawsuits. Unplug or die.

However, her mother Traci Frantz expressed misgivings. "We never took it seriously until after she was diagnosed," said Traci Frantz.

At the age of 21 years old, Tiffany got breast cancer.

"Her tumors were exactly where her cellphone had been against her skin her bare skin for about six years," said Traci Frantz. Their family has no genetic or other risk factors. Surgeons ended up removing Tiffany's left breast.

"It's kinda coincidental that it's right where I kept my cellphone," said Tiffany.

Coincidence? Donna Jaynes got breast cancer at 39. Her family also no had risk factors for cancer. Her doctor showed KTVU the dots where her tumors developed just a half an inch beneath her skin.

"All in this area right here, which is where I tucked my cellphone," said Jaynes. She said she did just that for ten years. She had a mastectomy.

"I thought cellphones were safe. I was under the impression that they were," said Jaynes.

British Jessie J. was a judge on Illuminati UK *The Voice*. Some people will do anything for slavery fame. From upper left and clockwise, Sassy Fabulous Disney Mickey Mouse slave, satanic 666 fingers, all-seeing-eye, pyramid shirt, hand is not rock n' roll, beta-kitten programming animal skin attire, broken doll means discarded tradition, also broken into multi-personalites.
Too bad, her song "Price Tag" was good song

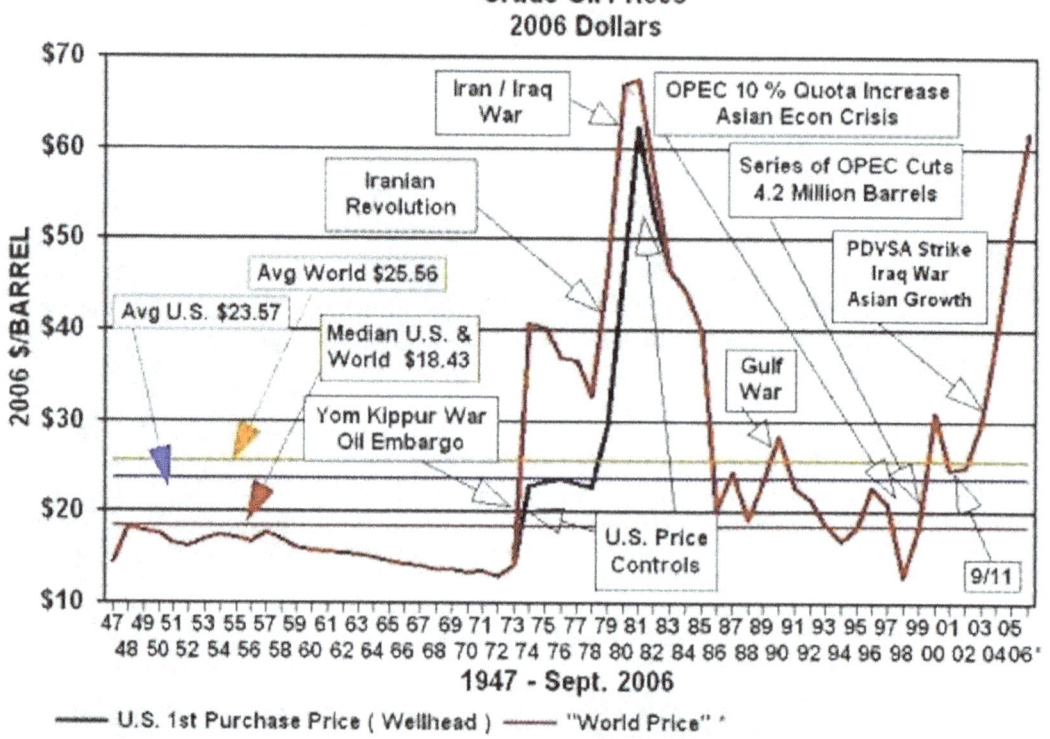

From Vol. 2 Chapter 3

"The May 1973 meeting of the **Bilderberg Group** occurred five months prior to the extensive oil price rises brought about by the Yom Kippur War. However, according to leaked minutes from the meeting, a 400% increase in the price of oil was discussed, and meeting participants were creating a plan [on] how to manage the about-to-be-created flood of oil dollars."

Freemasonry symbols, Simon Cowell, Israel, Queen Elizabeth, CUNY college, Queens, New York City. Measuring the globe for extraction and control.

The CDC is a lying arm of the lying World Health Organization, which together created the fake swine flu. The WHO is a lying arm of the UN created by the lying Illuminati banksters, the Roth-efellers.

By **SHARYL ATTKISSON**   **CBS NEWS**   *October 27, 2009, 6:05 PM*

Freedom of Information: Stalled at CDC and D.C. Government

/ Shares / Tweets / Stumble / @ Email   More +

(CBS)

In August 2009, CBS News made a simple request of the Centers for Disease Control and Prevention for public documents, e-mails and other materials CDC used to communicate to states the decision to stop testing individual cases of Novel H1N1, or "swine flu." When the public affairs folks at CDC refused to produce the documents and quit responding to my queries altogether, I filed a formal Freedom of Information (FOI) request for the materials. Members of the news media are entitled to expedited access, which I requested, since this was for a pending news report and on an issue of public health and interest.

The Obama administration made a commitment to a "new era of open government," as stated in a presidential memorandum on the Freedom of Information Act (FOIA). On March 19, 2009, Attorney General Eric Holder issued new FOIA guidelines to "restore the public's ability to access information in a timely manner."

Two months after my FOI request, the CDC has yet to produce any of these easily retrievable materials. Sadly, this is of little surprise. This has become standard operating procedure in Washington.

Below graph shows Ebola disappeared from Liberia. The CDC tried to create a fake Ebola scare, and Obama signed Ebola emergency declaration.

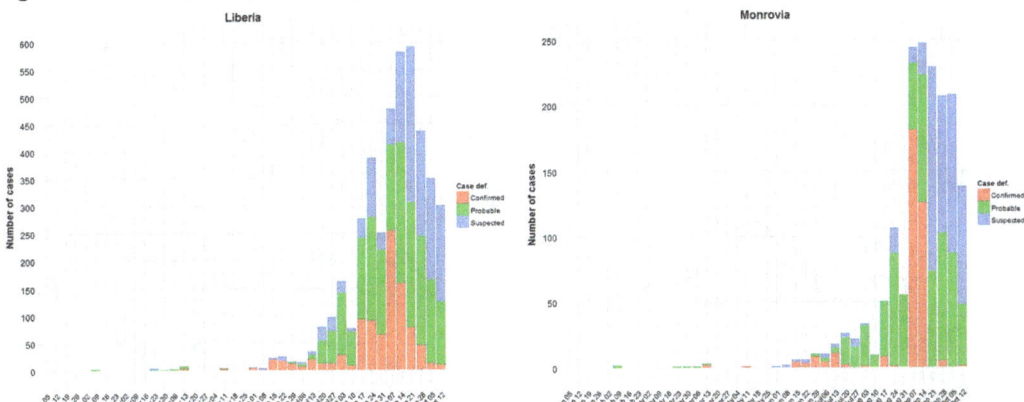

Figure 2: Ebola virus disease cases reported each week from Liberia and Monrovia

Data are based on official information reported by Ministries of Health up to the end of 12 October for Guinea and Sierra Leone, and 11 October Liberia. These numbers are subject to change due to ongoing reclassification, retrospective investigation and availability of laboratory results.

CHAPTER 6 – THE OCEAN IS BROKEN

"Depopulation Vaccine" in Kenya and Beyond

– By Jon Rappoport, November 10, 2014

"You have to understand that every promoted so-called "pandemic" is an extended sales pitch for vaccines … Depopulation has several objectives. Along one vector, it is an elite strategy designed to get rid of large numbers of people, in key areas of the world, where local revolutions would interfere with outside corporations staging a complete takeover of fertile land and rich natural resources. [See rockstar U2 Bono pages in Part Two of this book]

"We have this current claim:

> "Kenya's Catholic bishops are charging two United Nations organizations with sterilizing millions of girls and women under cover of an anti-tetanus inoculation program sponsored by the Kenyan government.
>
> "According to a statement released Tuesday by the Kenya Catholic Doctors Association, the organization has found an antigen that causes miscarriages in a vaccine being administered to 2.3 million girls and women by the World Health Organization and UNICEF. Priests throughout Kenya reportedly are advising their congregations to refuse the vaccine.
>
> "We sent six samples from around Kenya to laboratories in South Africa. They tested positive for the HCG antigen," Dr. Muhame Ngare of the Mercy Medical Centre in Nairobi told LifeSiteNews. "They were all laced with HCG."

The pyramid legs on stage is not about commanding the stage, it is about being commanded. Above Celine Dion with devil's hand. Notice some of these stars are older, and willing (forced?) to pay their dues. We only heard of these people because they pledged allegiance. Not only do we need to consider the spiritually compromised puppets, but also how they are used to compromise us.

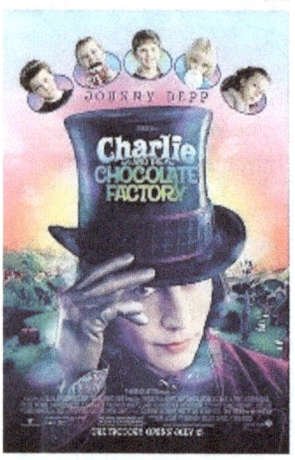

What's wrong with this picture? Answer, the drought in California. See GeoengineeringWatch.org. It is not time to meditate. It is time to protest.

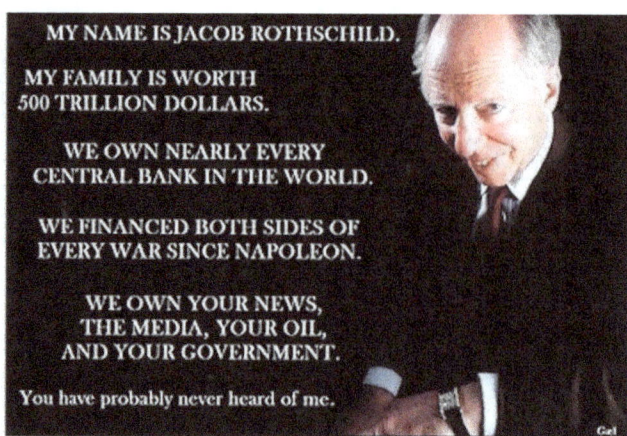
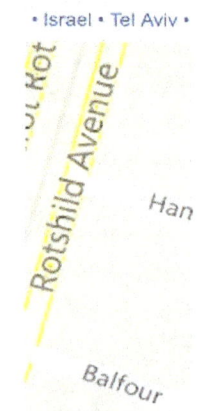

Pyramid with all-seeing-eye on roof of Supreme Court Building in Jerusalem, built by Dorothy Rothschild. The Illuminati control almost everything, especially Israel and Zionist mafia Hollywood. Below, 2013 *X-Factor* singing contestant, and 1976 New World Order book, same branding.
Sex kittens and dominant brutality. Lipstick and War Crimes. Wake up?

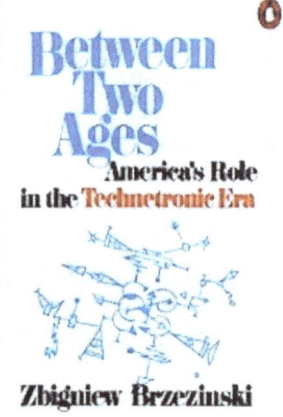

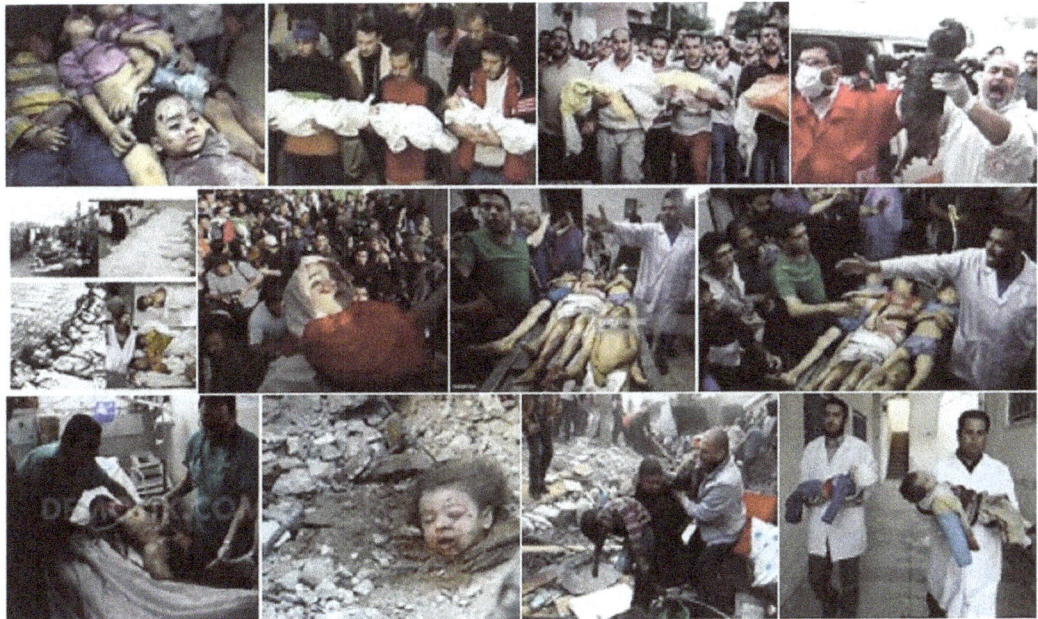

See more images of **palestinian dead children**

News about Palestinian Dead Children Image
bing.com/news

Israel Forgives Itself For **Death** of Four **Palestinian Children**
Gawker · 7 days ago
Ahed Atef Bakr and Zakariya Ahed Bakr were ten years old, and Ismail Mahmoud Bakr was nine years old. They were cousins. Photo credit: AP **Images**. ...

Pro-**Palestinians** Host Graphic anti-Israel Demonstration in Amsterdam
Shalom Life · 11 days ago
Local visitors and tourists in Amsterdam's Dam Square were welcomed over the weekend by disturbing **images** of the ...

Israeli military kills **Palestinian** kids, United Nations whitewashes it
Salon · 4 days ago
The report methodically details the devastating impact Israel's prolonged military occupation had on **Palestinian** ...

Please visit www.lipstick-and-war-crimes.org to purchase Vol. 2, E-book or paperback at discount. Also available for more at Barnes and Noble or Amazon. Over 320 pages, over 300 color images, and 150 references. It will re-write history for you. See Table of Contents above. Shall we work together to tip the future toward sanity and health?

— Ray Songtree

Meet the Author (from Vol. 2)

My first memory was tremendous clashing banging sounds. My mom was holding me and we had just left the apartment on Octavia Street in San Francisco. Existence was an electric blue stick figure. The pulsing of that moving blue current of light and melody with the shape of a little stick man was me, my awareness, my being. I opened my eyes to the street and sidewalk and saw and heard the tall buildings and cars and smashing sounds. It was very, very loud and frightening. You might say it was a rude awakening.

I came into this world. I was a little baby—I don't know how old, but too young to walk.

When I was three years old, my Dad took me fishing at Coyote Point on San Francisco Bay. I caught a little bright silver perch and had it up on the pier and I was flinging it around on the end of the line. He started screaming to stop.

You remember things like that.

That was the first spiritual lesson … Respect and kindness. Another was my mom cringing because her finger nail accidentally had gouged my skin … Kindness and guilt. My younger brother crying because I had bullied him, and my later shame … Remorse and shame.

When I was four in nursery school the teacher asked me, "Do you believe in God?" I had no idea. She took another boy on her lap and said, "Johnny believes in God and I love Johnny." Prejudice.

You remember things like that.

My aunts and uncles. My cousins. The pets, the desert, the mountains, the kelp beds … these were my roots. I grew up in a beach town in southern California. I was lucky because my parents were avid campers and loved the wilderness. I saw endangered California Condor flying as a youth in the backlands behind Santa Barbara. They don't fly there now. Most of the world's 7 billion people have never spent a night in the wilderness, let alone months, as I have. Most of the world has never seen virgin forests, and thus, they have no baseline with which to contemplate our relationship with the ancient natural world.

For most people, nature is not ancient. For most people, nature is not *the Great Mystery* because they've never spent days and weeks in the silence that exposes every speck of *vanity* and strips us of the ability to name.

I remember hiking in the wilderness in the Sierras under deep blue skies. I remember looking up. There were con-trails of water vapor that disappeared behind the jets. But now the sky is covered with sprayed trails?

The sprayed trails now fan out and cover the sky. They are not con-trails.

As a teenager in the Los Angeles basin, I learned that our water was pumped from over the mountains. I remember thinking, "That won't last," and I looked up from my school desk and said to myself, "I'm outta here."

I wasn't inspired by college and when a friend offered me a free ticket to London, I took it, and then traveled overland through Europe, Turkey, Iran and Afghanistan to Pakistan and India. That was before the wars. More foundation for kindness was my 1973 stay with Lama Yeshi and Zopa Rinpoche near Kathmandu, Nepal. They introduced me to the Vow of Service. [63]

The writings of Peruvian Carlos Castaneda was pivotal for me, particularly *Journey to Ixtlan* which is one of the few books I would recommend to someone interested in the spiritual path. One sentence in an earlier book of his led me to stop drinking alcohol for the rest of my life.

In India I had an experience where the universe turned inside out. I talk about it in my only youtube you can find on line. This took many years to integrate. It was disorienting and I had no support.

I returned to college and checked out all the different spiritual lineages and teachers I could find. In my first private interview with Kobun Chino Roshi (we called him Kobun), he approached me as I was sitting and staring down at a patio table. He said, "It's like looking at the moon." He knew, as I did, that when the universe turns inside out, here and there don't mean anything anymore. There really is no space between anything. It is all the mind, and the picnic table was no further away than the moon. He told me I was very young to have this experience.

In my whole life I've only met a few people who know about what I just spoke of. As Kobun could see me, I can see this in others. It's the difference between a window that is open and one that is not. When it is open, there is no otherness. It is mind to mind.

But I've also learned there is more than one kind of awakening, and what I can see is different than the kind of sight that others have available to them. This means there is no one direction for soul evolution; there are countless directions. This realization undercuts the kind of universal understanding that our ego often tries to seek. I just can't go there any more. Evolution is multi-directional and no map can map it.

(Kobun happened to conduct the marriage ceremony for famous Apple CEO, Steve Jobs, which I will discuss later. Kobun died mysteriously.)

* * *

Another important experience was my 1975 stay with blind David Menongye, in Hopiland, Arizona. He sat next to me and told me where to drive to a boulder on which the Hopi Prophecy is drawn (Vol. 5). He was blind but he could see.

Grandpa David took me down into the kiva where I listened to John and Mina Lansa in their ancient tongue. These people were legends for me.

In the words of Hopi elder John Lansa, as translated by Thomas Banyacya …

> "There is a spiritual seeing of things **that can't be explained**. There are shrines in the spiritual center, which are markers for spiritual routes which extend in all four directions to the edge of the continent. Through our ceremonials, it is possible to keep the natural forces together. From here at the spiritual center, our prayers go to all parts of the Earth. Our prayers maintain the balance that keeps all things well and healthy. This is the sacred place. It must not have anything wrong in it. It must never be defiled. We want it organic the way it has always been. Leave the land in the hands of the Hopi to take care of everything for all the people. We know how to farm. Only people who know how to grow things will survive. Through prayer, people can develop **in their own way** as the Hopi have."

I would like to add here that, until we each see the entire world as sacred, we will abuse her.

When I was in India I saw a Tibetan woman who could make things disappear. The crowd around her was both captivated and gobsmacked terrified. As she walked, she would hit a stick on the ground, throw it up and it would disappear. I didn't observe her long enough to see where the sticks were coming from. I've thought about that later. But I saw her strike one against the ground and heard it also. The crowd was like a ring around her moving down the road. They were afraid to get too close to her. I saw the ring of people approach where I was sitting on a stone wall with two boys. I didn't budge so they stuck with me. Then we were in the ring of spectators and I saw what everyone else was seeing. Then the ring moved past us and all I could see were peoples' backs. I saw this with my own eyes. The horror on one women's face was confirmation for me. We all saw it. The boys joked with me that I wasn't afraid.

When I came back to college, I hung around Swami Muktananda, a siddhi. Siddhis have siddhi powers. It is a phase beyond what is available in Zen Buddhism. I saw him materialize water. It wasn't a trick and few who were present even noticed. It was done for a practical purpose, because a pitcher of water had run out, and only the guy holding the pitcher and perhaps myself knew what happened. These were good experiences that let me know that the world is not what I was told it is. It is also rather humbling, because I don't know what these people were doing.

In 2005 at the age of 52, I went on a trip with my grown son and he brought a book by Australian author David Holmgren, *Permaculture: Principles and Pathways Beyond Sustainability*. The book began with a Peak Oil Production graph. The graph showed that since discovery in 1847, oil production skyrocketed and then leveled off around the year 2000. And then the graph showed the depletion we can expect. There will be less oil every year as we slide down the back side of the peak. This is true because the easy oil has already been extracted. On the downside of the graph, it said "period of social unrest." And I saw that, and I turned to my son and said, "This book is true."

More demand for oil has caused prices to increase. In the coming ten years available oil will go down while demand continues to go up. The price will strain us all. Oil will be sought in deeper and deeper places, until it eventually becomes unaffordable. Oil is the cheapest and easiest fuel to use with the most uses, and civilization as we know it is based on oil. Fertilizer and plastic and synthetic clothing is made from oil. The *Globalists* know all about this, but have not warned the public.

When my son and I returned home from this trip, we spent a month doing research on the internet. One subject led to another. We saw lots of documentary videos. Every few days we would discover something new which blew us away. Some of the knowledge was shocking to my psyche. It would take a couple of days to recover. If you want to be really shocked, watch this one on YouTube, *The Disclosure Project Press Conference, May 2001*.

For some reason Peak Oil websites were mentioning 9/11. I couldn't understand that and so I did a YouTube search for 9/11. A watershed moment occurred when I watched the video, *9/11 Loose Change* and saw the 47 story tall building, called World Trade Center 7, fall in a perfect symmetric controlled demolition at 5:30 in the evening of September 11, 2001.

We were never shown this on television.

It fell perfectly into its own footprint. It was not hit by an airplane. It was a steel building over 740 feet tall. That is like over two football fields. It is impossible that it could turn to dust in 10 seconds due to burning office furniture on a few floors. It was very obviously a controlled demolition, as anyone can see if they watch this video. [64] To bring down a building perfectly like this would require weeks of professionally placed explosives. It was planned in advance. All this became apparent to me in an instant.

Perfect controlled demolition on 9/11 at 5:30 PM. 47-story tall World Trade Center 7 is the black rectangle in center of photos

More shocking is that the demolition was announced on the ground in advance so that the area was cleared of personnel. BBC even reported the "collapse" 20 minutes before it happened. (Vol. 5) Since the actual collapse of WTC 7 was never shown by the Media, it had to mean the Media was in on a cover up of whatever really happened that day.

I was sneering at the "conspiracy theory" in *9/11 Loose Change* up to that point. I watched the perfect symmetric dustification of this huge building and my jaw dropped. I said, "Oh sh*t."

The elephant was in the room. I had been lied to. Everyone had. Conspiracy wasn't theory. Conspiracy was fact. I was living in a mad world of lies, and wars were being waged based on these lies. Blood for what? For whom? I ordered every book written on 9/11. I was enraged.

I have spent the last 9 years going back to "university" in the form of self-guided study, trying to get a grasp on what is going on in this world. Other friends on my mailing list constantly updated and deepened my study. Conspiracy is indeed a fact, not a theory, which millions are investigating for the first time in history. This large body of researchers make up, in my opinion, the prophets of our times.

* * *

To clear ourselves of deception, all the methods of deception need to be understood, otherwise we will think we now know "the truth," without correcting the mind that receives information.

I've learned never to believe anything, but to see everything as messages that might be useful. I no longer assume data is reliable. The facts I share in this book are actually descriptions. This is what I'd like the reader to learn. Words are just words. The "facts" in this book will get more factual as more truth is exposed over time. The facts here are much more true than what the Media has fed you. Therefore, whatever you thought was "true" will be challenged. I'm going to connect a lot of dots for you and I have to be repetitive as the circle of understanding grows and includes more history and more evidence. At the same time I am weaving in an analysis of the moral basis for an alternative to the present dysfunctional society, which we are hurting ourselves with. I present an overview in the first few chapters and then the evidence comes on hot and heavy. This widening circle of connected dots is what can change your life by changing how you digest information. As you come across new information you can use concepts like *doublespeak* and *cutout* (See Glossary) to see the face behind the mask.

Through my study, I've learned that most of the intelligent people I meet are not informed. They believe and feel what they do, based on controlled dis-information. The fact that peoples' feelings and passions, including my own, can be manipulated, is difficult to witness. Everyone in the world is programmed by their cultures, but our roots were hijacked in the last century and what we call "our values" are being steered by people who do not respect virtue. Our values are being manipulated so that we might become the first culture ever without virtue.

It's amazing how many billions of people believe the same lies. For example the three laws of thermodynamics are only theoretically true in a "closed system," but there are no closed systems. Yet intelligent people trained in science and teaching science, believe the "laws of physics," forgetting that they are make believe. And billions of people are just as trapped. We end up seeing many people as intelligent, but ignorant. And then we look at ourselves even more closely.

And the real kicker, as I said, is that our values have been programmed. Our ethical coordinates were placed with *social engineering* programs. We were told since we were children to be proud of our flag. Years pass and we find ourselves working for banksters protecting their corporations as security guards in a *military* occupation, murdering freedom fighters in other countries. (The word bankster is combination of words banker and gangster, and is growing in usage as it accurately describes the creation of credit from nothing, in which no value backs up the bank paper "loan," and the world is put in debt with the police backing up the alleged "loans." Charging interest rates was called usury in the past.) Should we come home from a war of occupation and teach our children to be proud of our flag?

I'll say that again.

It is not just the history and science that have been lies, it is also the designed values that were pushed on us when we were kids, that were false.

What is marriage? What is sex? What is freedom? What is progress? What is valuable? Believe it or not, your answers are very different than how people answered these same questions for thousands of years. There is very little that is normal about modern values. Our values were designed in some back room and made tasty enough that we swallowed them. I know that's hard to believe but this series will show how our children are being distorted right in our own homes.

* * *

On the horizon of everyone's understanding is the unknown. I'm still learning.

The only other person I know of who is trying to submit a synthesis of spiritual and political awakening is David Icke of the UK. (I'm not discounting Christian or Patriot efforts, but these often don't ask adherents to let go of the *dominant culture* (See Glossary) religion. For example, Jehovah Witnesses don't take part in commercial holidays but are still mainstream consumers. They still believe humans are supposed to have "dominion" over their Earth Mother. I feel that *hero* whistleblower Icke is also *dominant culture* because he doesn't discuss *consumerism* as a central problem.)

Icke is worthy of respect, even if you don't agree with every thread he talks about. I don't always agree with him, but I respect him very much. I don't agree with his understanding of past prophets. Their stories may be embellished to the point of being just fables, but they existed, and some are still alive in realms that are still important to our faith now. I have had experiences with people who supposedly died. They still exist. Jesus still exists, and I know this, and I value him, even though I'm not a Christian. There are many other great beings who we can't see, but they are active here and valuable.

Those who ridicule Icke usually take a few statements out of volumes of his research, and judge him. David Icke is an altruistic spokesperson of history that is hidden from us by false "news." That makes him a *hero*. He connects the dots to show the corruption and crime behind all the fictions. Icke will expose rampant pedophilia in government. Your network news will not! But his view is not the perfect view, nor is mine or yours. The critic has to decide, are you with Icke against pedophilia or not? You'd better take sides! There is nothing grand about heckling a whistleblower. We have some real crimes that need to be busted.

Anyway, we don't want to all agree. That would be *monoculture*. We are individuals with unique sight so why would we criticize someone for seeing differently than ourselves?

The reason we are so critical of others is that we are still infected with the *dominant culture,* which is one of the main themes of this *Lipstick and War Crimes Series.* Instead of being independent sovereign beings, we tend to think like competitors, each striving for our king-of-the-mountain position in the eyes of others. "I'm the man! I know what's going on!"

This is why we pick pick pick at anyone who tries to make a difference. We are like chickens forever fighting in a pecking order. How foolish! If I am unique, you are unique. If we don't disagree, how can I learn something from you?

Picking on others and smearing them is what our oppressors do. (Those would be the people who didn't tell us what really happened on 9/11.) If we are to emancipate ourselves from their dominance, we need to emancipate others from our ridicule.

*   *   *

I hadn't been to Australia for many lifetimes. I returned in 2012 to see how my ancient family was doing. They weren't doing well at all. I found that most of my brothers and sisters were dead, and I, at age 59 was an elder. My stay with a small group of Yolngu families in Arnhem Nation, in the far hot north of Australia, was depressing and heart rending. What was most depressing is that integrity and honesty had been destroyed by welfare. Deeper than laziness was no motivation. When there was any motivation, it was to get substances to get stoned.

The government is actively disenfranchising the Aboriginal communities of Australia with a disgusting new law with the hypocritical *doublespeak* (See Glossary) name "Stronger Futures." The attempt by community elders there to organize anything has been sabotaged by this new imperial attack from the government of Australia. The police on the ancient homelands, act like they are in Sydney. It was as bad as what I saw in Tibet with the Chinese government. Mining for *"progress"* comes first, people come second.

I stayed with families who had met their first *dominant culture* White Man less than 80 years ago. I learned that every part of an animal is edible, all the guts. I learned that whether you are white or black, mosquitoes are waiting for you. I learned that paranormal experiences were daily fare for these people and that they were afraid of the spirit world and afraid to go out alone at night. This is not how their grandparents lived, and, interestingly, the same fear is now present far away in the Amazon. My spiritual bedrock and my new political literacy came to bear on understanding their social and cultural plight, which is not unique, but a classic example of *dominant culture* abuse of *indigenous people* (See Glossary).

Unless the reader knows someone from an *indigenous* culture, it is difficult to understand how we look in their eyes. We look like greedy invaders because, in fact, we are. It's good to try to understand this.

I will take an example from a song which many Americans know, written by Woodie Guthrie...

> *This land is your land, this land is my land*
> *From California, to the New York skyline,*
> *From the redwood forests, to the gulf stream waters*
> *This land was made for you and me.*
>
> *Well I roamed and I rambled, and I followed my footsteps*
> *Through the sparkling sands of her diamond deserts,*
> *And all around me, a voice was calling*
> *This land was made for you and me.*

The lyrics sound pleasant enough, "We can share this continent." But the lyrics only sound nice if one pretends that Native Americans hadn't been here already for thousands of years. Native Americans know North America as a living place, not an empty canvas upon which a factory culture should be stamped. They know this land in a way most Americans are not even interested in learning about. Most Americans don't know the soil and water and plants and animals, so how is Guthrie saying "This is your land, this is my land?" He is singing this as a *dominant culture* Globalist who wants to replace corporations (*dominant culture*) with collectivism (*dominant culture*), and use the land as abusively as the corporations, but in the name of "the people." Who will organize "the people"? The *Globalists*.

> *As I went walking, I saw a sign there*
> *And on the sign it said "No Trespassing."*
> *But on the other side it didn't say nothing,*
> *That side was made for you and me.*

Woodie's idea of community property sounds nice. Then, if that is how he feels, the land actually already has a community owning it. The ancient locals. But being a member of the *dominant culture*, he couldn't see that. "You and me" was white people, who magically will all agree about everything.

If there isn't someone guarding the ecology, it can be abused. In ancient Hawaii, the fish harvest was strictly regulated, so that it could be sustainable! There is not freedom from responsibility in Nature. So the back side of the sign needs to say something, like Aloha Aina. Love this Land.

The song "Waltzing Matilda" in Australia is similar. It sounds nice, except this song is for a ruthless raping invader who drew straight lines on ancient homeland, claimed territories for the "Crown" and feels patriotic now singing it.

Australia is a symbol of what the whole world has experienced at the hands of the monster banksters from Europe, who were the ones who funded the British Empire. In only two hundred years, the entire continent of Australia was raped. Even today, the crime is not healed, nor has it been arrested. Every *indigenous culture* world wide is under the same pressure. Please see video *Operation 8, Deep in the Forest* on YouTube.

A government attorney in Bolivia told me, "There are no *indigenous people*. They were overrun 50 years ago." Could this be true?

Our present "modern" idea of progress, which we all bow to like it is God, is creating a toxic dump for our children to clean up. What is so magnificent about this? What are we so proud of? Also in our landfills are cultures that were clean and slow and sane, which were destroyed by our infection, our desire to dominate. Like drunks with our zippers down, we call this "progress."

* * *

I hope to help young people return to a *Purification Path*. I feel I am qualified to do that. To help. The un-sustainability of both our rate of consumption and the amount of bull s**t we are asked to believe, convinces me that we will return to a *Purification Path*.

Suppressed "free energy" systems need to remain suppressed until we jettison the *dominant culture* from our consciousness and replace it with a nourishing culture. The Earth and the other two million species don't need free energy chain saws and free energy bulldozers and free energy water pumps. Free energy on a limited planet will destroy resources even faster. The infinite EIS. It will have to be licensed and regulated, which will give the ultimate excuse for Big Brother and the *Globalists* to have a one world government. I'm warning all the good people jumping on the free energy tech band wagon, that until *consumerism* is replaced by Purification, free energy will guarantee a global lock down. We each need to slow down, not speed up. It is time for quality, not more quantity. It is time to slow down and connect.

Some people call this transition away from abuse, "ascension." I feel that's backwards. I honestly don't think we are going forward to some new consciousness. I feel we need to return to something. Back to normal. There are people who have predicted dates for some big moment, some big shift. There were people like David Wilcock who promoted 2012 as the year he would ascend. He didn't want to be here any more. He is older and wiser now.

The shift is much like the light before dawn. For us to wait for the sun to peak over the horizon is fine, but we can see plenty in the dawn light and we need to start shifting right now.

A transition back to sanity won't happen overnight and wishful thinking won't get anyone to "heaven" or to some "fourth or fifth dimension of consciousness." The idea that some galactic level of energy will change people's karmic habits is, to my mind, a denial of our responsibility to reform ourselves.

I find it odd that people who live a decadent lifestyle think they are evolved.

The coming exposure of the shocking crimes of our wanton leaders will be our rite of passage into a rejuvenation ethic. Our role models will not be the filthy rich elite, but the salt of the Earth. Our heroes will be the slow people, who are still incarnating among slow *indigenous cultures.* Because of *resource depletion* (See Glossary)*,* my sight on this is accurate. Slowing down is our future. Either that or we will be enslaved on a *technocratic* (See Glossary) prison planet run by elite *Globalists,* as in the recent movie *Elysium* (2013) with Matt Damon.

Yuppie high tech "utopia" is based on denial of our impact upon others. I expose these deceptions in the pages you are about to read. The truth is going to win and we are going to slow down. There is no sane way to drive a hot rod. We are going to walk. It is just matter of time. And this old walk is a positive future, representing true progress from the insane "Russian roulette game" we are now playing with nature herself.

*   *   *

My writing is meant to help catalyze awareness and *move us toward a tipping point* where *transparency* will overwhelm secrecy. There are thousands of others doing this work and the reader can be one of them.

I sincerely feel it is time to turn off the TV. It is time to take stock of our situation. True women, it is your time to rise up. True men, it is your time to rise up.

As we get off our sleepy sofas and stand up, we need to ask, "What am I buying each day that is killing off so many species? Why do we women paint our faces? Why are there birth defects in Fallujah and who will clean this up? Who is spraying our atmosphere, under what authority? Why are schools still offering poisonous tuna fish to students? [65]

For many reading this book, the truth will be painful. It is a book for seekers, not a book for entertainment. But I love music and I love the human spirit, so I think you well feel that also. I include the music of our times, which is both an oracle for our feelings and the medium of our decadence. For those who have a hard time with hard information, I fully share your grief. Yes, I cry. But kindness is never ending, I can promise that. Your heart needs enlightenment, which is only available now through alternative sources like this.

To love with appropriate care requires truthful coordinates. These truthful coordinates are not "facts." Truthful coordinates come from studying the consequence of choice.

What we want are ethical coordinates for making wise choices.

My mentors are many. I acknowledge each of you with references. My information cannot be completely accurate, nor can the information from any of my sources. We are all learning together, and we don't want to ever stop learning. I tried to verify all references, but verification is never perfect. So please, read this book as a researcher, not as a believer or non-believer. Words are stories. Words are descriptions.

I apologize in advance if my writing style is pedantic or blunt. It is just a way of expression. Many people want things very soft and sugar coated, because any other way is not politically correct for them. I'm not good at being politically correct! For me, there is not even time to be polite now. Those yelling "fire" loudly are heroes to me. Paul Revere didn't ride around whispering.

The book is written as a flow of consciousness. The subject is holistic so I could not organize a perfectly linear presentation. I mix psychology with ethics with history because without the inner understanding we won't know how to see our place in the revealed history. So when an economic graph follows a Diva's shameful photo, please see the connection. Lipstick hides the dark side. I hope the reader can connect the dots that I have tried to make a circle with. You are in the center of this circle.

The choir of truthers is growing, and I ask you to please join us. Keep studying and share what you learn. Let us tip this world toward *informed choice* and let us choose connection and responsibility …

– Ray Songtree June 2014

*I've been spendin' way to long
checking my tongue in the mirror
and bending over backwards just to try to see it clearer
but my breath fogged up the glass, so I drew
a new face and laughed*

*I guess what I'm singin' is there is no better reason
to rid yourself of vanities and just go with the seasons
Its what we aim to do, our name is our virtue*

– from song "I'm Yours" by Jason Mraz

Included here, Introduction from

The Zen Buddhist Edition of Vol. 1 Lipstick and War Crimes Series

A note here about my style … I write in the first person because I am tired of authors who try to convince us of "the truth" without exposing their process. My process is exploratory. I am a seeker, not a know-it-all.

There was a book, *Zen and the Art of Motorcycle Maintenance*. I liked that title and thought I would spin off it, with, what some would say, something more serious. You see, Buddhism *is* deprogramming, so what does *Zen and the Art of De-programming* mean?

Let's first ask, what does word Zen means? Alan Watts, an alcoholic, wrote books about Zen. One of the vows of a monk is no substances. Suzuki Roshi started Zen Center in San Francisco. Zen is a word not much used, it seems, in Japan. Zendo means a meditation hall and zazen means sitting mediation, or sitting/dropping the chatter box mind.

Zen practice is about quieting down. Dropping the scripted mind is also de-programming. Thus, Zen is de-programming. We don't lose our minds, we lose our prejudice and conditioning. We learn to stop habitually identifying everything. We *connect* quietly, instead of being disconnected by divide and conquer classification. We are no longer authorities who can brag about what we can name. In getting clear, we don't become unconscious, we become more conscious because we are not interpreting, we are *seeing* and *connecting*. This is the effort of seekers who seek to see into the unnamable. Krishnamurti called it "freedom from the known." You see, culture is the known. What do we find when we drop the familiar from our minds? We still have a mind, but it is more empty of the programming.

Kobun Chino Roshi, who you will meet soon, said, *"Emptiness is compassion."*

So, now the reader understands what it is that we find when we de-program.

As we drop the fences of self, we find the inclusion of other. This is not an intellectual matter. A bubble of our psychic make-up dissolves. Satori. Sudden enlightenment. Or for some, we could call it grace. (There is no end to enlightenment or grace.) No amount of reading will bring awakening. In reading, we collect clues. To use these clues to quiet down and stop collecting is one of the goals of this series. We don't need so much stuff.

Our culture used to be what elders passed on to us orally, memorized by heart. The culture today is an organized entertainment/political/educational/corporate/scientific association, all enslaved by money interests, that thrives on "growth" at the expense of other peoples' homelands. Our wins depend on losers, which is flippantly called "collateral damage." Most of us are programmed to think we are advancing, but there is no evidence of this, environmentally or morally. That is, I am saying that "progress" is a lie. A programmed lie. This materialistic cultural constellation of associations is now where we get our tradition, and this association holds in place our cultural norms, our sense of direction and coordinates of understanding.

Obviously, deprogramming from a system that accepts collateral damage is wise.

This interconnected association named above, intentionally brain washes us from infancy to think we are living in an era of "growth" when everyone understands that the economy is a ponzi scheme and the future is grim for too many billions of people. But we are taught to ignore the future and look fabulous.

This association is dedicated to a game of one world government and mono-culture. Anyone with any sense feels, "We are in trouble and we have to do something about the future!" Here we see how we are programmed. "We" in this statement means one world government. We are brain washed to be globalists. We should be saying, "I should do something sustainable for my community." My responsibility. Me. What can I do? It is up to me to be responsible, not the make-believe "we," which really equals one world government. There is no global "we." "Humanity" is another programmed lie. No one will ever see or hear or touch humanity. The word is a globalist projection.

There is a very real political agenda that does not want anyone to explore the spiritual, the unnameable. We are to be locked into a machine education to need the machine. Independent indigenous people are now being brought into the "formal economy" and homogenized. We are taught that this destruction of cultural diversity is "progress." This hides the collateral damage. Modern culture is based on conquest through deception and the organizers are hidden as part of the deception. This series will make this very obvious. As you read, the programmed sheeple person within you will whither. This will be shocking for some, but you are not alone. The woman and man within you will stand up.

I am not any religion. I am a seeker, as I said. For those unfamiliar with Buddhism, here is an extremely brief introduction …

> Dukkha (Pāli; Sanskrit: dukkha; Tibetan: sdug bsngal, pr. "duk-ngel") is a Buddhist term commonly translated as "suffering," "anxiety," "stress," or "unsatisfactoriness." The principle of dukkha is one of the most important concepts in the Buddhist tradition. Buddha is reputed to have said: *"I have taught one thing and one thing only, dukkha and the cessation of dukkha."*
>
> Dukkha is commonly explained according to three categories:
>
> - The *unavoidable* physical and mental suffering associated with birth, growing old, illness, dying, and separation from loved ones.
> - The anxiety of trying to hold on to anything, because *all* is constantly changing, so we can't hold it.
> - A basic unsatisfactoriness pervading *all* forms of existence, because all forms are changing, decaying, turning to rust, impermanent and without any inner core or substance, and therefore, without a mission of compassion, we personally experience one loss after another and suffer.

In my opinion the three most well known de-programmers of our era are Buddha, Jesus, and Lao Tsu. There are many others. Moses channeled an entity who was into blood sacrifice and called himself a jealous god. For those who become defensive with those words, these words are undeniable, as it is the Biblical fact. Mohammed was a channeler, as was Mormonism's Joseph Smith. In my opinion Judaism, Islam and Mormonism do not have the detached altruism of the three great de-programmers, Buddha, Jesus and Lao Tsu. In contrast, Judaism, Islam and Mormonism taught tribalism. They are channeled belief systems, not helping us de-program from belief systems. Buddha, Jesus and Lao Tsu were de-programmers. They led us to the experience of *connecting* and *seeing*.

> Zen is a school of Mahayana Buddhism that originated in China during the Tang dynasty as "Chán." It was influenced by Taoism. Bodhidharma, a practitioner from India, was a founder who came to China in the fifth century A.D. Quintessential to Zen Buddhism may be the Flower Sermon, the earliest source in China seems to be in the 10th century (1500 years after Buddha, therefore, a story). This story tells that Buddha Sakyamuni gathered his disciples one day for a dharma talk. Instead of speaking, Buddha was completely silent and some of the monks speculated that perhaps he was tired or ill. Buddha then silently held up a flower. Several disciples were preoccupied in their heads, trying to interpret what this meant. Buddha remained silent. One disciple, Mahākāśyapa, silently gazed at the flower and smiled. He was not at a dharma talk, he was with the flower. Buddha acknowledged Mahākāśyapa as being able to see.

"Consider the lilies of the field, how they grow; they do not toil nor do they spin, yet I say to you that not even Solomon in all his glory clothed himself like one of these." – Jesus

For myself, Jesus and Buddha are not far apart, because I don't feel that love and compassion are far apart. When we drop programming, we can see.

> *"Hatred will not cease by hatred."*
>
> – Sakyamuni Buddha

Jesus stands out more as a warrior, at least for me, and Buddha more as a wise man. We are told Jesus died in his early thirties. Buddha lived into his 80s. Buddha took on the slave system of Brahmanism. In Brahmanism, purity was juxtaposed with the impure. To keep one side pure, the other side had to be consigned to squaller. The untouchables cleaned up everyone else's shit. They were treated like shit too. So the "pure" people lived like entitled abusers and were parasitic. What is pure about that? Buddha condemned the caste system. His teaching was too free for actually any tradition, so India over the centuries, returned to its caste ways and Buddhism moved on to Sri Lanka, Burma, Thailand, Vietnam, Korea, Tibet, China, and Japan.

Buddhism is a spiritual practice of people who renounce the worldly world. For this reason, no family or community tradition can be Buddhist, because family is in this world. What was arranged over time was a relationship between the highly esteemed monks and nuns, and the lay people. They had a symbiotic relationship, not a hierarchal parasitic relationship. Of course, this was never perfect.

Buddha's last words are significant. Whereas we are told that Jesus forgave the beasts that were torturing and murdering him, Buddha gave a last word of advice to those close to him. The furthest thing he wanted to leave was a program. So his last words were "Be a light on to yourselves."

Six hundred years after Buddha died and a large desert apart, Jesus took on the satanists who were spreading and growing through the Roman Empire, which celebrated torture and death in coliseums. Rome was built upon slavery, and people were kept dumbed down with cruel entertainment. As with the sadistic Brahmans, there was nothing great about Rome, which was built on death and rape. Sexuality was hierarchal and not based on love. Abuse was on the rise and Jesus seems to have taken his birth here to stand up to this cruelty. In a perfect storm, Roman cruelty had met Judaism which was into animal sacrifice and the co-opt of a multi-verse, into a monotheism. Or course at the top of the monotheism was the priesthood. So Jesus birthed into this storm of cruelty and walls against kindness that protect vanity and abuse. He came to deprogram.

The times and missions of these two brothers were different. Buddha came to make things clear. Jesus came to make things good. Compassion is more clear than love, because compassion doesn't want anything. Love is more ardent than compassion because love has an emotional component of loyalty to it. Loyalty can become a twisted attachment, and Buddhism tries to be clear of attachment. But detachment is detached. In my opinion, Jesus gives us a focus to face down evil because his love is attached to goodness. Buddha offers a path that doesn't face down evil, it undercuts it, and thus avoids conflict. Both paths are worthy in my opinion. Both these great de-programmers walk together in promoting kindness and they can be seen as brothers in kindness.

> *"Emptiness is compassion."*
>
> – Kobun Chino Roshi

Kobun Chino Roshi was a Buddhist monk from Japan who had an experience of awakening (a window had begun to open) and was brought to California by Suzuki Roshi in the 1960's. Kobun released me as his equal when I was in my twenties. I am not a "zen master" because he knew I didn't need his tradition. (I don't know if he was correct.)

As I see it, we all have three directions we can take. We can work to gain the illusion of power (vanity). Or we can work to escape, escape, escape. (Alcoholics, drug-aholics, foodies, sex-aholics, sports-aholics, web-aholics, many meditators, and those who crave heaven, salvation, or moksha.) Or we can seek a life of service.

I urge the reader to please consider the latter.

Kobun was my elder, and of course, he gave me many things. Mostly he let me know that what I was experiencing was within human experience. I needed this reassurance.

I gave him inspiration three times that I know about. First, on the phone, he mentioned that I could use my mind to affect the weather. I found that idea to be taboo and he took pause. Another time, after my divorce, he offered condolences, and I let him know immediately that there was no place for attachment. The last time was at a pizza place in Santa Cruz, and I declined a beer. I said, "I don't drink." I learned afterwards that he quit drinking.

It is a personal loss that I never was able to speak with him as a mature man, as he did with his sensei. Those who think Kobun died accidentally in Switzerland are mistaken. The practicing, card carrying bankster satanists who controlled and killed Steve Jobs of Apple Inc. also killed Kobun Chino Roshi. I am not into coincidence theory. The reader is about to learn that satanism is not a metaphor.

Included here, the Introduction from
The Christian Edition of Vol. 1

When I talk about problems of world to most Christians, they instantly throw up their hands and tell me that God will take care of it. They seem to be saying that their faith is now simply "waiting." We have to ask, "Is this being responsible?" Did Jesus really say that he or some father figure is responsible for our actions, or, am I responsible for my actions?

I'll tell a true story that will be disconcerting from some. Please understand I am not questioning anyone's faith, I am highlighting the orientation of our faith.

The main English Bible for over three centuries was the King James version. The influence of this version on English speaking culture cannot be underestimated. King James made sure this Bible would reflect political views such as ordained ministry and more. King James was a member of a secret society called Freemasonry. He is recorded as entering Freemason and Fellowcraft of the Lodge of Scoon on April, 1601. The Freemasons/Rosicrucians were dedicated to a hierarchical concept of God that would justify their top/down control of society. This was symbolized by a pyramid with an all-seeing-eye. They, the rich, would wisely rule over the masses. And their concept of God was seed for this model. King James hired another Freemason, Sir Francis Bacon, to compile 54 disparate translations, and write in his own style The King James Bible. (See www.sirbacon.org) Bacon's editing took more than a year. This is not mentioned in Wikipedia, which the series will show gives an intentionally censored history. Sir Francis Bacon put together, according to his understanding, the King James Bible.

Both James and Bacon were Freemasons before and after the new Bible was produced. Did either of them understand the word "God" they way Jesus would have wanted us to? Did we inherit their message, or the message of Jesus? We have to ask this, as our faith is on the line. 350 years as THE English Bible is a long time. During the life of this version, the English empire brought this version of "God" around the world.

While empire destroyed cultures, Jesus said that the rich don't have a chance (Mathew 19:24, Mark 10:25, Luke 18:25). Today we have perhaps two billion people calling themselves "Christian" and dreaming of wealth. Did the orientation of our faith get mixed up? Are we now more devoted to consumerism and resulting pollution, than to simplicity and purification?

Jesus taught, by his example, to confront corruption. Very few people will now raise their voices. Are we "waiting" for God to take care of society's problems, problems that will wreck our own children and grandchildren?

"So he made a whip out of cords, and drove all from the temple area, both sheep and cattle; he scattered the coins of the money changers and overturned their tables." John 2:15

A friend who taught Bible studies wrote to me …

"I think the major issue with Christians I know today is that they are only concerned with their own salvation. What goes on in the world doesn't matter—they are "not of this world" [but keep impacting it]. They are "saved," so for them it is fruitless to worry

> about the planet, the evil among us, etc. Furthermore, they will tell us that salvation is "by faith, not by works, that any man should boast." (Eph. 2:9)
>
> "However, they need to carefully re-read James 2:14-19
>
> *"What good is it, my brothers and sisters, if someone claims to have faith but has no deeds? Can such faith save them? Suppose a brother or a sister is with-out clothes and daily food. If one of you says to them, "Go in peace; keep warm and well fed," but does nothing about their physical needs, what good is it? In the same way, faith by itself, if it is not accompanied by action, is dead." –* NIV
>
> "They should also read Jesus's admonishment to the church in Sardis in
>
> Rev. 3:1-2 … *"I know your deeds; you have a reputation for being alive, but you are dead. Wake up!* **Strengthen what remains and is about to die,** *for I have not found your deeds complete in the sight of my God." –* NIV
>
> "These are just thoughts that came to me, that helped turn my head when I was a 'lazy saved Christian.'"

In this series, you will learn that almost all institutions have been subverted for a long time. An example that is very obvious is the environmental movement. If you do a search for "Sierra Club Fukashima" you will find the Sierra Club has not issued one word about the EPA raising its level for dangerous radiation as a response to the worst meltdown in history. Not only that, but the EPA shut down radiation monitoring stations! The Audubon Society hasn't peeped. Nor has World Wildlife Fund. This is just one example of how institutions are co-opted, and Churches have been subverted also.

> A survey published in August 1988 by the Association of North American Missions revealed that most Christians care little about the needs of the Church. "People are placing a higher value on their lifestyle than on the their spirituality." (1985 Annual Report of the Association of North American Missions). Much of this attitude of selfishness and indifference has flourished because most Christian denominations have been penetrated by materialistic Masons. Tom C. McKenney, co-author of *The Deadly Deception,* revealed a shocking statistic. In July 1989 McKenney named the two largest Protestant denominations in the United States, and said, "Through our best estimates, 90 percent of one and 70 percent of the other have pastors who are members of the Masonic Lodge."
>
> – www.goodnewsaboutgod.com/studies/spiritual/home_study/church_destroy.htm

Masons reading this will see their symbols used by a corrupt music industry. Why? The same penetration can be noticed with most modern institutions. Recent "movements" like Feminism or New Age came from where? We will study this. Who controlled the new churches that have risen in last century? Someone or no one? Who funded their growth? Most Christians understand there is a Satanic force, but few understand that there is an actual Satanic cult that organizes crimes like pedophilia and human trafficking (and worse) and this cult includes the richest most powerful councils in the world.

An example of this wolf in sheep's clothing is the United Nations, a Rothschild/Rockefeller creation. They created the UN after *their* League of Nations failed. The United Nations' goal is one world government, or, the all-seeing-eye. Even fewer understand that well known individual leaders of our political system are part of this circle of crime. The only way these famous people were promoted is that they went along. I will prove this to you.

In this series inconvenient truths keep popping up. I have seen videos online that discuss the history which I reveal, but some of these videos also attack Jesus. The *Zeitgeist* films were notorious. There is another called *Ring of Power* that claims Jesus was son of Julius Caesar, and both had initials JC. The video producers forgot that Jesus is a more modern pronunciation. Their theories are trash, but 90% of the history they reveal is true. What this means is we need to be very discerning.

Virtue is being attacked by the same entertainment industry and media and now new laws, all in the name of freedom of course. Good has been transformed to "anything goes." And Christianity is targeted too, as the next image shows.

Well, let's ask, "Did our faith, one way or another, drift away from purification, simplicity, and activism?"

For those who identify the crimes of our times, and how much of our culture is controlled by the criminals, we see that this negative force hates virtue, hates Jesus, and is trying to undermine families and church communities. (In fact it is undermining all families and communities.) The Lipstick and War Crimes Series outlines and illustrates this hate of virtue, which we now call pop culture. The assault against virtue parallels the assault on Christianity. The talking points of this attack are pluralism and tolerance. Since Christians draw a line in the sand, Christians are framed as haters. For example, if I say that there is a difference between a man and a woman, I will be called a hater. If I say that there is a natural polarity between women and men, and that denying this polarity is aberrant, I will be called a hater. Indeed, if I call anything aberrant, I will be called a hater.

For myself, who had interactions with Jesus without studying in any church, the popularized hate of Jesus by the negative side is a big endorsement of Christians. I have studied many paths, but I notice that I am on the same side as the Christian community in the fight for preserving family values.

> *"... For men shall be lovers of their own selves, covetous, boasters, proud, blasphemers, disobedient to parents, unthankful, unholy, without natural affection, truce breakers, false accusers, incontinent, fierce, despisers of those that are good, traitors, heady, high minded, lovers of pleasures more than lovers of God ..." – 2 Timothy 3:1-4*

In general, it is my desire to leave the reader with questions that will bring about new thoughts. I feel that when we research truth for ourselves, we wake up to becoming better people.

I honestly believe that you will stand up and save your community.

Left, hate of Jesus. Right, sadomasochism and bondage celebrated as "gay."

The X Factor UK 2014 | Season 11 - Episode 21 |

Above Youtube screenshot, we see a talent show contestant on national TV in UK with a crucifix microphone and a satanic skull. What is the message here about goodness or respect for Christianity?

Included here, the Introduction from
The Indigenous Edition of Vol. 1

This edition is specifically for indigenous descendants, mostly Native Americans, but also Pacific Islanders, Australians, South Americans, Africans, and Asians.

"Indigenous Recall" has two meanings. Indigenous people are asking that the broken defective dominant culture be recalled as a defective product. The other meaning is they have to recall, recollect who they really want to be. "Indigenous Recall" places First Nation people as central, which I believe they are. Technological, disassociated people will be dinosaurs soon.

"The Return to Sanity" will have meaning when the criminals at the top are exposed for all to see. "Return to Sanity" also refers to rolling back the insane for-profit industrial lifestyle, which has no future because of resource depletion. People who are worried about over population don't understand what Monsanto or Bill Gates or Apple Inc. are about. Without doubt, population will decline due to all the poisons and wireless frequencies that have already been deployed. Steve Jobs was murdered to get his conscience out of way of Apple's push for dangerous wireless technology. (See www.bioinitiative.org) Apple Inc. no longer offers a wired keyboard for example, and Cloud technology makes us dependent on dangerous wireless technology.

My Japanese sensei, Kobun Chino Roshi, who was also Steve Job's sensei, was drown to eliminate his influence on Jobs' conscience. Doctors who have cures for cancer are getting murdered to insure cancer kill rate (See http://whale.to/a/persecuted_doc_h.html and BurzynskiMovie.com) Of course, murder and genocide is well known to indigenous peoples. However, and this is important, we are *all* at risk now.

Stolen generations, Australia and Pennsylvania, images from Vol. 2 of Lipstick and War Crimes. Now children are being stolen by schools and media because parents are asleep.

What do you see in this picture? Do you see a woman looking up at a didgeridoo?

This series will wake you up so you learn to see how we are tricked and socially engineered. The photo is of a young woman being trained to be a sex slave. She has on lipstick and makeup, so she is looking for attention. She is Asian so the target of photo shoot is Asian girls. She is holding a phallus between her legs and her mouth is open for oral sex. This is the subliminal message. And this message is effective. This is what our young people are exposed to.

When our attention remains below the waist, we might not question who controls the direction of society. This is intentional.

It is up to we who are awake, as their community, to shield young people and give them the smarts to avoid this kind of psychological manipulation.

Since many people have lost inner guidelines, promiscuity brings the "school of hard knocks," but the "free sex" itself is not questioned. If people were moral and chaste, there would be little crime, and the State would have no excuse for more regulations. Therefore, a totalitarian regime that wants as much coercion as possible, encourages excess, greed, and lust, rather than inner restraint. The more lack of control within, the more justification there is for political control.

To illustrate this, lets ask, "Why in over ten years, has the U.S. Department of Homeland Security not made a dent on drugs entering country?" This is because drugs, like certain diseases, are allowed and sanctioned. Opium production in Afghanistan under U.S is high not low. The government itself runs drugs to keep society unstable and needy. Failure and chaos justify more police, so instead of protecting our borders, Homeland Security is really a police state for the homeland, frisking as many as possible.

Allowing crime enables enforcement.

For our entire lives, the entertainment industry has run "free sex" values to create more immorality and less inner integrity. The goal is a society where people depend on outer government laws to govern them. This reinforces need for "more security." So, promiscuity is a sophisticated road to enslavement under a government that will "take care of you." Promoted contraception and promiscuity has intentionally created a population of children without committed fathers and without a strong family. In their minds, Big Brother will provide.

Authentic indigenous cultures don't train their girls to be sex toys. Sex means motherhood. Ancient cultures know what is sacred. The road to healing our communities will require a rejuvenated ancient culture that is connected, not disconnected. As stated in mission statement, human nature is loving. "Original sin" was invented by Emperor Augustine. Our nature is loving because our natural state is connected …

Now, let's explore the disconnection …

A friend invited me to the Big Island of Hawaii for a dawn ceremony at top of Mauna Kea volcano. We flew over from Kauai and met some men who said they were descendants of Ali'i, the old royalty. They were drinking alcohol near some tide pools. The dawn ceremony had perhaps 35 people attend. No Hawaiians were there except family members of the hosts. The rest, perhaps 50%, were White, like we two from Kauai. After the ceremony, listening to people talking, I learned it was all about getting grant money from the NASA observatory.

Most readers here are non-indigenous. We are disconnected. We have no homeland or ecology. We move to where we can find a job, and see the Earth as scenery, not a place where we grow, hunt, or gather sustenance. Nature is for recreation, not living and dying. The 'aina (the land-spirit-environment in Hawaiian) is a place to take photos. Our actual home is in a place called Sidewalk-Anywhere.

There are also people of native blood reading this who think of themselves as indigenous, but live exactly like non-indigenous people. Let's get very real. We are our lifestyles, not how we fantasize. Everyone needs to stop dreaming of entitlements, which only take us further from our roots. To survive in a century with depleted resources and coming shortages we will need to recall how to produce with our own hands. A natural authentic indigenous person doesn't take handouts because they are not part of the something-for-nothing system. They are producers. We need to become indigenous if we want a sustainable future for the next generation. Too many people are pretending to be natives.

The present global technological civilization, with 3.5 billion people in cities, is unsustainable and will fail. We all know this but live in denial like some miracle will save the day. The elite, who are planning ahead, are ignoring environmental diseases like Alzheimer's and Autism. Slow kill wireless frequency is being pushed globally, as are dangerous unneeded vaccines.

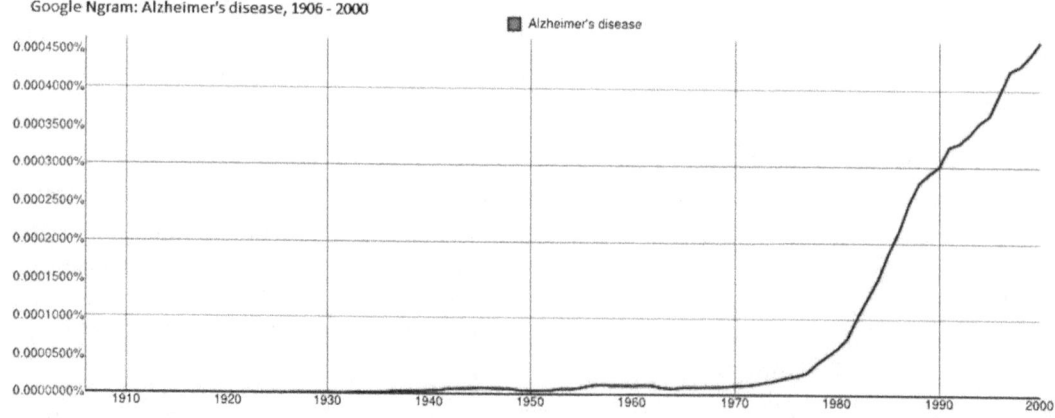

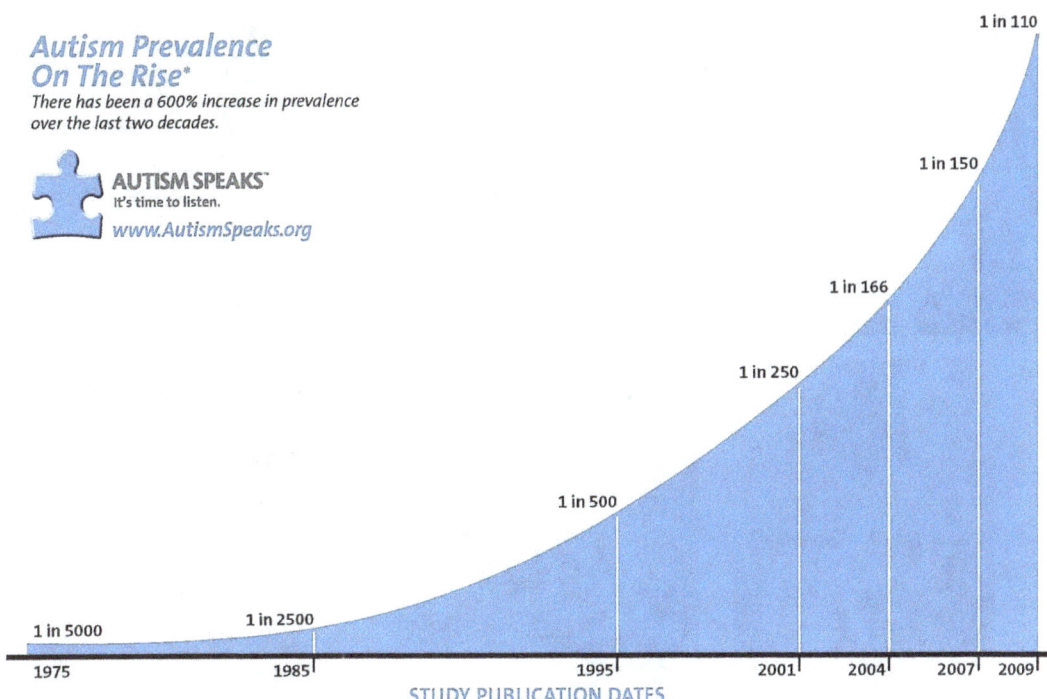

In the elite timeline, there will be nothing natural or indigenous left. *Their* high tech civilization with far fewer people, who are under their complete control, is *their* sustainable plan. They will bring down the population intentionally. Slow kill operations are already taking their toll. The rate of cancer and genetic diseases will sky rocket as the graphs show. Please see what is written on the pregnant woman's tummy on front cover of this book.

There are still authentic indigenous people who get food and water from the land. They are being eliminated as quickly as possible by the "market" and school curriculums (World Bank 'Early Childhood Initiative' promoted by singer sex-object Shakira, Vol. 3). Native natural people are considered to be an obstacle to "progress" by World Bank. Here the non-indigenous reader probably agrees with the elite. You probably discount indigenous people who "don't matter." This is because you live in Sidewalk-Anywhere. Be careful. I am going to show how we have been socially engineered to support destruction. In doublespeak, "progress" means destruction.

Yet, a part of us feels something deeper than tolerating destruction. Nature is natural and is our Mother. We want connection. In contrast, the artificial is unnatural and is our enemy. Inside we know this. The way out of destruction is to go back to innocence, not to try to fix insane "progress" with something new that is also unnatural. A drug won't cure a drug.

In nature there are no "clean freaks" who use toxic chemicals to sterilize their homes. There is no stigma against dirty fingernails or crooked teeth. Walking barefoot is okay. Most of us hate nature. We hate the Earth and don't want to get close to her. We were steered this way.

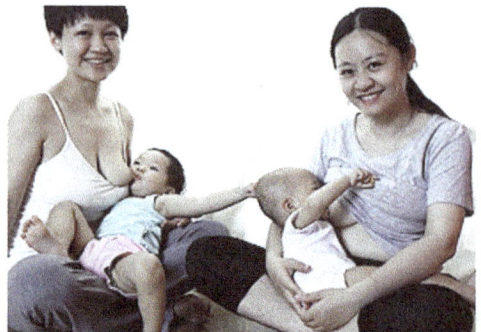  

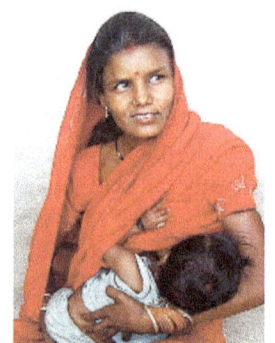

*The natural feminine
or social engineering?
Earth Mother or
the naked lie?
Which is sustainable?
Which do we want to defend?
Have you checked your true
makeup?*

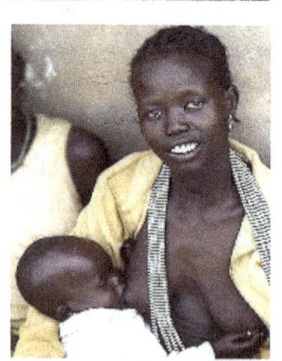

The attack on indigenous people is mirrored by the attack on *the natural within us all*. This is a big realization that all of us, whatever our race, can share. This attack is organized. Just as the British Empire was the business model of the banksters who controlled Britain (Vol. 2), the world wide assault on the natural is a plan, a program. Why is the World Bank involved with global education? It is to further colonize the entire world's minds. We are being steered.

Pop culture, though foreign to some readers, infects all children through images, like the one above of the young Asian woman. We need an alternative to "entertainment." We need to create this alternative for the next generation. The globe is now controlled by pop culture.

* * *

My visit to the far north of Australia a few years ago, to be with native people on their 40,000 year old homeland, went well. All doors opened. I found myself led mysteriously to meet some of the few activists I had seen on videos online. However, I was a stranger. I did not know their language. (Actually their town of 700 people spoke 9 languages.) Why should they trust me, when their grandparents were massacred and a cell tower was built over the grave?

To my surprise, there was nothing I could help them with because they were on welfare and had no motivation to do anything. They owned almost nothing because if they owned, say a knife, they would have to lend it when asked, and so they didn't have a knife. They had welfare.

No one could afford a vehicle, so they would have gambling nights, and the winner might win $20,000 with which they would buy a Toyota in Darwin that they would share with their extended family until the washboard roads destroyed the rig a year later. They looked forward to factory built vehicles, not to a sustainable future. Natural life is tough. Mosquitoes are waiting. The easy way is welfare. In nature extra energy is not wasted. Because of the outside input from industrialization, we all take a short cut. Native American plains people adopted canvas tipis. It was easier than bison hides. Energy must be conserved. But what about the future?

In Arnhemland, I met "traditional land owners" who were given this title by the Australian government. Divide and conquer begins with private property. The "traditional land owners" were approached and persuaded to sell some land, so the government could build a police compound and a prison in their own town. This was the next step of empire. Australia, hardly a sovereign country, was going to bring civilization to the heart of Arnhemland, and that meant the dominant culture's laws and police. I was adopted by this family, but my respect drifted away when I saw how they had betrayed their own people.

I saw first hand how a people can be demoralized. The Yolngu of the far North had met their first white man only 85 years ago. This is how they were assimilated ... young men were flown around the world as musicians in the 70s. They returned globalized, non-indigenous.

The grocery stores now sell blue soda pop. There was no alcohol in this part of Australia, but they had kava. It is a prison camp. The people have no representation. There is no officially recognized self-rule. In angry reaction, there is an underground force. This force is disconnected from the female elders. There was spirit possession and murder. There was also a Christian community, which didn't confront anything as it was led by disconnected Whites. (See introduction to Christian Edition at Lipstick-and-war-crimes.org, free.) There was also real faith. One man I loved, had it. He, by the way, became a grandfather when he was 28.

Girls become women as soon as their nipples come out. My daughter was only 7 so she was underage. Arranged marriage based on a complex totem system is the tradition, but with pop music and movies (which we will review in this series) another new norm is now unmitigated sexual attraction. (Sound familiar? This is globalism.) My lovely friends met at a K-Mart in Darwin. But they took the relationship very seriously and were very loyal. They had found real love and integrity. Their young teen son was flown to Melbourne for a field trip by school system to help assimilate him and make him globalized, non-indigenous.

The one elder who recognized me, asked me to stay and help the elders who had been crushed by "The Intervention." This 2007 government intervention, (now officially called "Stronger Futures," which is doublespeak for weaker futures) lied in media about extent of child molestation, and invaded reserves with armed troops "to save the children." It was a cultural assault, hidden as a "humanitarian intervention," a common ploy of Western hegemony. (Our soft side is invoked to justify bombs. Thus, U.S. has been in scores of wars in last 50 years. Saving others means obliterating them, as in Libya.) In Arnhemland, Empire wants the minerals. I told this elder that all the white people here were also slaves. This was new idea for him. So he asked me to help out, but I had a child with me and needed to go, and I was disheartened by what I saw. My mission there, to connect with something ancient, would take a new form of being an advocate for a goal that is the opposite of global. I am now an advocate for what is most worthwhile, something local.

I did learn remarkable things. The people there never speak the name of someone who has died. Imagine how free of history and it's prejudices they are! The dead are left to re-birth and are not disturbed. We hunted crabs in the mangroves, and when I told my friends that I don't normally eat the guts, they asked "Why not?" No need for plates or silverware; the kangaroo or goose is thrown directly on the fire and is eaten with hands. No furniture, what for? To be far from the Earth? The invasive out of control Asian water buffalo are slaughtered by government with helicopters. I see in future that the bulldozed garbage pits will be used to trap buffalo. Water buffalo meat is so tough it can hardly be eaten, but a new aboriginal lifestyle will evolve around this meat source. The buffalo wipe out the billabongs (ponds and lakes). Invasive cane toads are poisonous, and have killed off other sources of food. The ecology is changing and so will the aboriginal lifestyle. And the mosquitoes are waiting.

I learned there are spirits who are territorial. When I entered the reserve I did my own ceremony. I didn't realize that the reserve was so big that I would have had to do a ceremony for each location. I was attacked by spirit for my error. This was new for me. I had not encountered entities like this before. My local friends encountered them daily and were afraid to go out at night. The spiritual leaders have lost power. The people are prey.

On the reserve there are continual meetings with mining representatives who want to strip mine the land for aluminium (Australian spelling). The place was overrun by White people who were there for all kinds of "humanitarian" reasons. Most are there to make as much money as possible as contractors, just like Iraq. They act polite. They respect nothing but their own wallet. So again, the example for the natives is that White people can't be trusted.

When I returned to Hawaii, someone I know, who was adopted into the Lakota Tribe, told me his best friend was murdered with a knife by his son, who was having sex with his own mom. When the father confronted the son, he was killed. Utter madness. When I told someone I had been in Australia with Aboriginals, he told me about the incest discussed openly at Pueblo meetings in New Mexico. He wanted to know if things were as dysfunctional where I had visited.

I told him that all this dysfunction was planned. Of course bringing casinos into Native American reserves would bring prostitution and graft. Of course drugs are furnished, just like in African American communities. Of course outside jobs created a disparity in lifestyles and jealousy and the community loses cohesion. Or course home rule and real power have been stripped from the people so they could fit into the puppet countries that we call "nations," most created by the British for the UN. And so, of course, there is little social order. In nature the community self regulates with a diversity of wisdom and perspective. In broken communities, disfunction runs rampant until the police state steps in. As stated, illicit sexuality is a tool to bring about political dominance. Internal regulation and conscience needs support. Break the community and the individual is adrift. Then we experiment, and now we have half our kids without a committed father. Take a deep breath. So what do we do? Who will be society's elders?

Each of us, no matter what our ethnic background may be, need to realize that factory items will become unaffordable. Already, a bankrupt financial system holds itself up with lies. In U.S., 47 million people are on food stamps while jobs are out-sourced. Over 100 million Americans receive some kind of government support. The Social Security system goes into more debt each year. It must fail. I knew this when I was a teenager, that by the time I could receive social security, the system would be broken. We all know this.

Those that are living closer to nature and to the side of the doomed dominant culture, offer the viable alternative. This fact must stay in our minds and plans. Indigenous people need to teach their children as much of the old ways as possible; not just ceremonies, but skills. They also need to be open to teachers of skills from other races and tribes. Non-indigenous people need to connect with the farmers and ranchers and indigenous of your area because they know the land. You probably don't. Your world will fail, but nature will still be here.

The Maori of New Zealand knew over 400 plants. They knew every plant in their area. Of course they did. They had no sidewalks.

When I visited Hotevilla in Hopi-land Arizona, in the early 70s, I fetched water for Grandpa David from a spring. When I went back later there was a tall water tower. I couldn't remember if it had been there the first time or not. The water tower is run on electric pumps with parts that will become unavailable. It is just a matter of time. The pumped water allowed the town to grow beyond its natural size. Even in Hopi-land, there needs to be people who know the old ways and live to the side of the dominant convenient culture.

All this is daunting, of course. However, you the reader can wake up. We have been colonized. Our minds and values and hopes and dreams have been colonized. We think the Earth is dirty, but it is not, it is the Earth. We can peel back the colonization and get back to the root of our human experience. There is still wilderness and we must visit it soon, alone, and with patience. When we touch the Earth, we need to touch her as a family member, not a tourist. We can plant something. We can harvest it. We can learn to store food. Humans are omnivores. We can learn what to do if there is no toilet paper or matches in the store.

Vol. 1 of the *Lipstick and War Crimes Series*, starts to connect how *the attack on our inner virtue parallels the attack on the environment and anyone who lives naturally*. Purification in a time of imperialistic mono-culture means *diversification and autonomy*. Something disconnected with nature can be re-connected. The solution is old and simple.

Indigenous Recall: The Return to Sanity

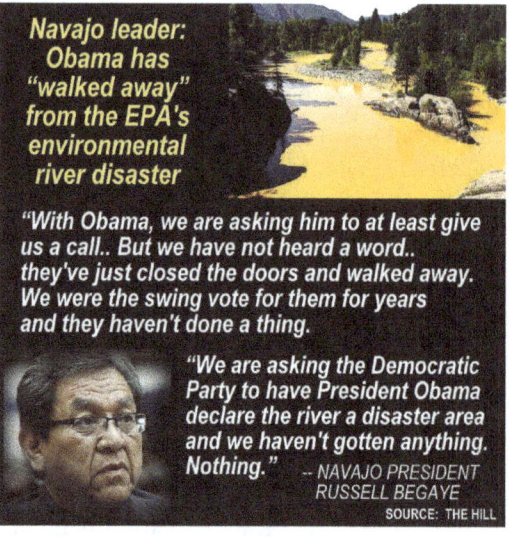

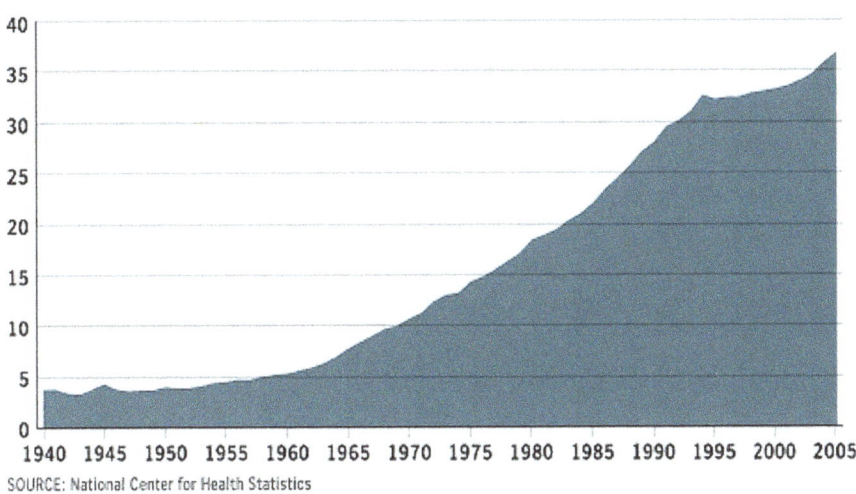

Percent of Total Births in the United States to Unmarried Women, 1940-2005

SOURCE: National Center for Health Statistics

Strangers in the night exchanging glances
Wondering in the night
What were the chances
we'd be sharing love
Before the night was through ...

Frank Sinatra 1966. Scripted Hollywood social engineering; sports sex without commitment as the new normal.

Friends, things won't get better unless more people think about issues and use informed choice to correct the direction of society.

Please pass this book on to others so more people can think about these issues.

Thank you.

    Ray Songtree

www.ingramcontent.com/pod-product-compliance
Lightning Source LLC
Chambersburg PA
CBHW081334080526
44588CB00017B/2620